1621 ⓞ

Operation Portland

Operation Portland

The Autobiography of a Spy

by Harry Houghton

Rupert Hart-Davis London

Granada Publishing Limited
First published 1972 by Rupert Hart-Davis Ltd
3 Upper James Street London W1R 4BP

Copyright © 1972 by Harry F. Houghton

All rights reserved. No part of this publication
may be reproduced, stored in a retrieval system,
or transmitted, in any form or by any means,
electronic, mechanical, photocopying, recording
or otherwise without the prior permission of
the publisher.

ISBN 0 246 10548 8

Printed in Great Britain by
Willmer Brothers Limited, Birkenhead

To
Ian and Dorothy

Contents

1	Insecurity Service	1
2	Black Market, Warsaw	6
3	Drink and Diplomacy	16
4	Recruited	26
5	The Truth About Crabb	43
6	Meetings and Landings	53
7	Enter Gordon Lonsdale	67
8	Microdot to Moscow	81
9	Breaking In	86
10	Closing In	95
11	'D' Notice in Reverse	115
12	Longer than Life	124
13	The Blake Penance	140
14	It's Cold Outside	154

'This has been a case which by its very nature has been full of intrigue. You may say it has all the characteristics of what is called a thriller.'—Lord Parker, addressing the jury in his summing-up of the Portland trial.

Chapter One

Insecurity Service

One Autumn afternoon in 1960 two anglers were placidly fishing in a lake at Wisley, a few miles from Guildford along the A3. Nearby was the Hut Hotel, where two other men had just arrived to spend the night. After tea the newcomers strolled down to the water's edge. What more natural than for them to stop and chat with the fishermen?

There weren't many other people about. The rods were placed so that no-one could have got within earshot unnoticed. It was a good place for an uninterrupted conversation if you had secrets to discuss.

And the four men did have secrets to discuss. The anglers were called Roman and John. They were genuinely interested in the sport, and often fished here for relaxation. Today they weren't altogether relaxing. The other two men were Gordon Lonsdale and myself. We were, all four of us, spies.

It was a nice innocuous setting for a meeting. We had plenty of time, and nothing to fear. Our inflexible rule was that nothing of an incriminating nature should be carried on such occasions: we were here simply to discuss a project, the details of which would have to remain in our heads.

The project was a proposed break-in at the Underwater Detection Establishment at Portland.

I now know that some of us were already under surveillance by Special Branch and MI5. But not that day. Nobody in the Security Service knew about this crucial meeting, or about what followed. There are so many things they didn't know, and never have known up to this minute.

When they finally did catch up with us, the Lord Chief Justice said as he passed sentence on the man who used the name Gordon Lonsdale:

'I take the view in this case that yours, so far as the activities of the five of you are concerned, was the directing mind.'

In most subsequent reports Gordon was referred to as the masterspy. In fact, what Gordon knew about naval matters could have been written on the back of a postage stamp—and I don't mean in microdot. He hardly knew the sharp end of a ship from the blunt end, let alone anything about the sophisticated machinery inside. All he did was pass things on—from me for transmission to Moscow, or to the leader of our group, or from the leader to the rest of us.

After my release, Superintendent George Smith, who had led operations against us, said to a newspaper reporter that it was nonsense to claim that the head of the conspiracy had not been caught. 'No-one else,' he asserted, 'was involved in the ring.'

Another newspaper contradicted this by stating that Whitehall knew Lonsdale and the Krogers weren't heads of the spy ring, and identified the leader as a former first counsellor at the Soviet Embassy.

Both views are dead wrong.

The Security Service did a painstaking job, and we were trapped in the end. But if only the pains they had taken had been just that bit more intensive, they could have wrapped the whole thing up a lot sooner and made a much more spectacular catch. An awe-inspiring number of agents, identified in Court only as B, D, X and so on, delivered statements which gave the impression of a whole regiment watching our every move and listening to our every word over the better part of a year. Yet they failed to follow up several important leads, including the most significant they were ever offered; and when at last they hooked us, they let the big fish get away.

It was stated that I had been closely watched from February 1960 until the day of my arrest. I can only say that they let a lot of supposedly vital material pass unimpeded through our hands during that period, and that if I had been watched at all attentively between 3rd and 7th September of that year the remainder of the gang might have been tracked down, and the trial would have proved an even bigger sensation.

At the trial Witness B, an officer of the Security Service, told of his duties on a day in July 1960. His report makes interesting reading. He records that I met Ethel Gee at the Cumberland Hotel and took her to the intersection of Waterloo Road and The Cut to meet Gordon Lonsdale, with whom we exchanged greetings which made it clear that we were 'well known to one another'. Lonsdale then took something white from his wallet and handed it to me; I, a few minutes later, gave him a carrier bag in which was a parcel wrapped in brown paper.

It sounds just like all the best spy stories. In fact, so far from the three of us knowing one another well, it was the first time Miss Gee had ever met Lonsdale, and she never knew him by that name. The 'something white' consisted of two tickets for the Bolshoi Ballet. The carrier bag contained a plastic mac which he had left behind when last visiting my cottage.

An agent who trailed me over a large tract of Dorset and Hampshire made great play of a mysterious cardboard box on the back seat of my car. The way the statement was read out, it seemed to add one more sinister link to the tightening chain of evidence. In reality the box was merely one I kept in the car to carry groceries in.

One has to admire the meticulous detail of it all. But while all this sort of thing was being recorded, think of what they *missed*!

A really crucial report was prepared by an agent who, with a colleague, followed Gordon Lonsdale and myself into Steve's Restaurant in Lower Marsh, again near Waterloo. They sat at a table close to us. In all fairness I have to admit that we hadn't the slightest suspicion we were being overheard: that much of their job they knew.

What they heard was an arrangement for us to meet on the first Saturday in each month, with particular emphasis on the first Saturday in October and November at Euston. This the agent duly recorded. He also quoted more conversation which couldn't possibly have taken place. Lonsdale was supposed to have said, 'We'll use an interpreter,' which was absurd, since all of us in the group spoke English; and I am quoted as saying, 'I don't want paying yet,' which is even more improbable—I've never been one to decline payment.

The inexplicable thing is the failure to follow up that clear lead on the Saturdays. They had been given it on a plate. Yet under cross-examination the witness admitted that he never went to Euston. Nor, apparently, did anybody else.

There can be only one reason for this. Gordon Lonsdale had left the country for a holiday behind the Iron Curtain. The authorities knew this much and, believing him to be the ring-leader, decided his absence must rule out any meeting on the first Saturday in October. So they ignored the tip-off. Even on their own reckoning this was incredibly slipshod. A meeting between myself and *someone* had been clearly intimated, and although the supposed remark about the interpreter was either a mis-hearing or a wild invention, the senior sleuths weren't aware of this and had every reason to suppose a new face would come on the scene—perhaps two, since who would the interpreter have been interpreting for? It was a foolish blunder, stemming from the even more disastrous blunder of assuming that Gordon Lonsdale was top man and that in his absence nothing could happen.

It was my intention on being released from prison to settle down and forget as far as I could this discreditable period of my life. Other people haven't made it easy for me to forget. During my early days in prison I was repeatedly questioned by Special Branch men wanting to wheedle more information out of me, and when Miss Gee and I came out we were hounded by reporters and cameramen. Every time an espionage story breaks in the newspapers, as in late 1971 when large numbers of Russians were expelled from Britain, my telephone starts ringing and old half-truths and outright falsehoods are raked up. Bunty and I have been asked to write articles and even books according to a formula laid down by the editors and publishers concerned, showing how misguided we were and how sinfully we profited and how repentant we now are. Neither of us is interested in commercial concoctions of this nature.

Gordon Lonsdale is dead. Peter and Helen Kroger, in my opinion involved only by virtue of their skill as communications experts and doing no active intelligence-gathering themselves, are in Poland. Bunty, who believed right to the end that Gordon was an American called Johnson and who, in spite of accusations in Court, never received a penny for her part in our activities, knew nothing about the wider ramifications. So I am the only remaining member of the Portland Spy Ring in a position to tell the story in full.

I have tried to avoid what is already known about the case, other than summarising a few facts where necessary to keep things in the right perspective, and sorting out some misconceptions. I prefer to concentrate on what is *not* known. In his account, Gordon had to pull his punches in order not to jeopardise the early release of the Krogers. None of the defendants is now in prison: Gordon was exchanged for Greville Wynne, the Krogers for Gerald Brooke; and Miss Gee is now Mrs Houghton and we have completed our sentence, so I can speak without fear of putting others at risk.

In the Parliamentary debate the day after we were sentenced, Mr George Brown declared from the Opposition benches:

> The very size of the catastrophe that has happened in our counter-espionage and security agencies really does not seem to

have been matched before. I do not wish to exaggerate, but on the other hand we cannot acquiesce in whitewash being applied which may lead to us not seeking out what is wrong and putting it right. We are not only considering Houghton and Gee but the Krogers and Lonsdale—and all the other Krogers and Lonsdales who have not been brought into the net and about whose operations there appears to be a good deal of evidence. A professional spy ring of a very high order moved into Britain some years ago; those who came in 1954-55 were caught. Those who came before were not known and it looks as if Houghton had been in touch with the ring before then.

Lord George-Brown has not always been one hundred per cent accurate in his pronouncements, but in this instance he wasn't far off the mark.

I am sorry it happened. I am more than sorry I got Miss Gee (as she then was) involved. I'm also sorry that the concept we've always had of the scrupulous fairness of British justice and its complete independence from political pressures should have been so badly sullied during the proceedings. I make no excuses for myself. My sentence would probably not have been much different whatever happened. But convictions of Gordon Lonsdale, the Krogers and myself could have been obtained without such petty perversions of the truth, and without the unscrupulous refusal to allow us adequate defence facilities.

Bunty says of her own years in prison: 'I deserved every day of them for being such an idiot.' She is more forgiving and more philosophical than I am. I can't be so calm: a fair trial would never have led to that savage sentence on her.

It's time to tell it all as it really was.

Chapter Two

Black Market, Warsaw

I was born in Lincoln in 1905. Though my two brothers and I never went barefoot, I had numerous cousins who did: I think the song *There'll Always Be An England* must have been inspired by our family, there were so many of them.

I wasn't much more than a kid at the time of the Russian Revolution, but I remember the jubilation at home whenever a Bolshevik success was announced. Although not all the family were Left-wing, my grandfather on my father's side was a founder member of the Fabian Society in Lincoln, and my father's first question when we bought a cat's-whisker wireless set—always called 'the wireless' then, never radio—was: 'Will it get Moscow?' On my mother's side they were mainly Liberals.

We used to be taken as children to a working-men's club in Flaxton Gate in Lincoln, and instead of calling 'Time' the steward always struck up *The Red Flag*. My mother once told me that in naming one of my brothers Ivor she understood it to be English for Ivan, and as a matter of fact my grandmother would call him nothing else. Maybe poverty gave us an inclination towards the Left. Although my parents did their best for us, there's no doubt that we were poor. I still have recollections of going to see my Grandmother Houghton sitting at a scrubbed white table in the Workhouse in Burton Road, Lincoln: in spite of having so many sons and daughters, she had to suffer that indignity.

Is all this an explanation, or an excuse, for the ease with which I slipped into working for the Russians? I've done my best to be honest with myself about this, and I really can't find any political motives in what I did. Maybe some psychiatrist could dig down and find all kinds of hidden resentments or sufferings or something: but if he succeeded, it'd be quite a surprise to me.

I left school when I was fourteen, and two years later signed on for twelve years in the Royal Navy. After training I served in a gunboat on the China Station where, according to some recent writers of fiction masquerading as fact, I spent most of my time smuggling opium on such a scale that, if one-tenth of what they said was true, I could live in luxury for the rest of my life. Of course I dabbled in a few rackets here and there. I never knew a serviceman who didn't. The day you join up there'll be someone to tell you that 'the only crime is being found out'. The fact that I rose to be Master-at-Arms, the highest rank attainable on the lower deck, doesn't speak well for the wisdom of my superiors if I'd really been doing a Fu Manchu act in any exceptional way. Like later accusations of drunkenness in Warsaw and Portland, these smears dreamed up years afterwards show only that once you've been convicted for any crime in this country, profiteering hacks and public bar gossips accuse you of every other vice under the sun.

As things worked out, I stayed on in the Navy until 1945, having had some rough times on convoy duty in the Mediterranean and on the Murmansk run during the war...and also having had some rough times during my marriage.

I met Peggy a little while before the war, when I was on leave in Lincoln after paying off HMS *Aphis* in Shanghai. She had a baby daughter, Margaret, and gave me to understand that she was a widow. When my leave was coming to an end I suggested she might come to Portsmouth with me, and soon we were living together. It wasn't a very satisfactory situation, especially for her, and I felt we had either to marry or call the whole thing off. I really believed I loved her, and thought she loved me. We were desperately poor in those days: my pay was only four shillings a day. Marriage would mean entitlement to the Naval Marriage Allowance of seven shillings a week. It doesn't sound much now, but in those days it could make all the difference. Still Peggy hesitated. It wasn't until I threatened to put an end to the whole situation that she consented to marry me.

There was one proviso. She wanted to forget she was a widow, and marry in her maiden name of Smith. I didn't get the point of this, but thought it was a womanly whim and didn't want to raise any objections.

Baby Margaret was too young to know that I wasn't her real Daddy, and grew up regarding me as such. It wasn't until many years later, when she required a passport, that Peggy had to break the news to her that I wasn't her real father.

After demobilisation in 1945 I was taken on as a Civil Service clerk in offices connected with Portsmouth Dockyard. Within five years I was established as a clerical officer. I was now living at home all the time, and things weren't working out too well for Peggy and me. I've no doubt there was blame on both sides.

One or two imaginative writers have depicted Peggy as a poor browbeaten girl many years younger than myself. I never did discover her correct age, but as a married woman during the First World War she must obviously have been a lot older than I was.

As things between us got worse with the passage of years, I was tempted to call the whole thing off: but if I had taken steps to end the marriage it would have involved us in a lot of trouble, and I couldn't bring myself to go through with it. At the same time I couldn't stand much more of this cat-and-dog existence, and let it be understood that, while I wouldn't make any public show of it, I intended to lead my own life in future.

We put on the best act we could in front of other people. I know the truth seeped through to some of our friends, though usually embroidered somewhat: Peggy surreptitiously confided in them that I wasn't treating her properly and that all the faults were on my side. As to what I was doing with my free time—well, moralists may condemn me, but after the home life I'd endured for so long I felt fully justified in seeking happiness elsewhere; or, if not happiness, at any rate distraction.

Then we were offered a change of scene.

To maintain the fighting efficiency and mobility of the Fleet in the years when Britannia unquestionably ruled the waves and the Royal Navy was a force to be reckoned with, there were naval dockyards abroad in Gibraltar, Malta, Trincomalee, Singapore, Hong Kong, Simonstown and Bermuda, to name only the principal ones. These dockyards employed large forces of local labour, with home dockyard personnel in supervisory posts. When one of these home personnel was about to finish his service, volunteers would be sought for the forthcoming vacancy. The Foreign Service Allowances going with these posts ensured that there was never a shortage of applicants.

I had applied for nearly every vacancy in my own category. This wasn't merely for the sake of the extra cash but because, like many others who have spent years in the RN on foreign stations, I was finding it difficult to settle down to life in everyday England. Hearing there was a vacancy for Naval Attaché's clerk at the British Embassy in Warsaw, I even applied for that. I'd have preferred a job in a warm climate, but I was getting restless and the allowance for Poland was very attractive.

Regarding that one as rather a long shot, I went on to apply for another vacancy in Singapore. Then, to my surprise, I was invited to attend an Admiralty interview for the Warsaw posting.

I duly presented myself before a small committee of Admiralty civilian staff in Whitehall, where I learned that the entire naval staff in Warsaw consisted of one Captain RN and his clerk, the Office being responsible to the Director of Naval Intelligence. There was the usual 'We'll let you know' when I left the interview. It had been a day out at the Government's expense, and I thought to myself that this was probably all it would ever amount to.

A couple of months later I was informed that I had been selected for the appointment and was to prepare myself with the usual TAB injections and a medical examination. On being pronounced fit I was transferred from the Portsmouth office to Naval Intelligence at the Admiralty for instruction in coding and decoding signals, and other aspects of my future job.

Which was how Peggy and I came to find ourselves ranging the Hull docks one afternoon in search of the United Baltic Company's ship *Baltavia*, due to sail at 4 pm. The taxi driver didn't know where she was berthed. Neither did I. It was a Saturday and there was no one to ask. We got on board, a bit breathless, with about fifteen minutes to spare.

Then Peggy began to jib. The ship was about to sail, but she didn't want to go. I could go off to Poland on my own: she wanted to stay at home. I had to argue her out of it. A few of our belongings had already been shipped to Warsaw, most were in store, she had nowhere to go, nothing to sit on or sleep on. She talked of going to stay with Margaret, now married and living in Portsmouth. Finally the ship sailed, and Peggy was still with me.

After all this, the trip over the North Sea and through the Kiel Canal into the Baltic was comparatively uneventful. We arrived at Gdynia and my first experience of Poland.

No sooner had the *Baltavia* secured alongside the wharf than the crew, with the sole exception of the Captain, were ordered to assemble in the fore well-deck. Peggy and I, the only passengers, were requested to remain in the saloon while a thorough search of the ship was made by frontier security guards and dogs for possible stowaways. It was a bit baffling. There were plenty of folk longing to get out of the country, but I can't imagine who'd have stowed away to get *in*. Nevertheless the search took about two and a half hours.

In the meantime we were being formally and very correctly interviewed by Polish immigration officials in the saloon. All wore military uniforms and sported revolvers. We were eventually declared fit to enter the Polish People's Republic, and after a great deal of hand-shaking with me and hand-kissing with my wife, our interrogators departed. The search of the ship completed, the crew were dismissed from the well-deck. Armed sentries, both male and female, were posted on the dockside at short intervals along the full length of the ship, with another at the foot of the gangway. There they would remain until she sailed again.

We left the next morning, when the Consul sent his driver to pick us up and put us on the train for Warsaw. It was then that I realised the acute food shortage prevailing in the country. The steward of the *Baltavia* had provided us with packed meals for the journey and, having eaten lunch, I was about to throw some orange peel out of the window when my arm was seized by a woman who indicated in sign language that she wanted it. I couldn't understand why anyone should want orange peel until an English-speaking Pole in the compartment explained that oranges were hardly ever seen in Poland and that the skin could be used for flavouring. I felt pretty mean about this and wished we'd known before leaving the ship, as we could have brought enough for everyone in the compartment.

It was some sort of commemoration week, and during the railway journey I saw more pictures of Joe Stalin than I'd ever seen in my life. Every station was bedecked with the red-and-white national colours of Poland, and hundreds of huge photographs of Old Joe smiled benignly down upon the line.

At Warsaw we were met by the daughter of the Naval Attaché, who was vacating his post the following week. She took us to the flat we'd been allocated, and immediately departed, saying she was late for a party but would see me in the office in the morning. She explained briefly how to get there by tram-car, though I doubt if she had ever deigned to go on a Polish tram herself.

The flat was spacious enough, but almost denuded of furniture. There was only one electric light bulb in the place; there were two single beds with blankets; the gas had been cut off at the main, and no-one had bothered to have it reconnected for our arrival. By striking matches I discovered a massive range which would burn wood and coal, and a little coal to get it going. After a long delay we were able to make a cup of tea.

The next thing was to get some more light bulbs. I went downstairs to find the *dzorza*, or concierge. She was an old crone about eighty years old. I later learned that she hated the English, since the last occupant of the flat had been sent back to the United Kingdom by the Polish Government as *persona non grata* for spying activities. I could of course speak no Polish at that time; she didn't speak English, and flatly refused even to try to understand sign language. I came away empty-handed and with the knowledge that so far as she was concerned we weren't welcome at Clogera—the name of the block of flats. There was nothing else to be done that night in this utterly strange country but to transfer the one existing light bulb to the bedroom and go to bed. We had arrived; and I wasn't all that impressed by the reception.

Next morning I coaxed the fire alight in the range and made a pot of tea. Then, in my ignorance of conditions in Poland at that time, I took Peggy in search of a restaurant where we might get breakfast.

We went without breakfast that morning.

After fighting our way on to first one tram-car and then another, we found the way to the Embassy more by luck than judgment, and were greeted:

'Hope you had a good journey. Everything comfortable?'

I'm afraid my reply didn't augur well for future friendly relations.

We discovered that the Embassy had a shop, and stocked up with provisions. Most of these were imported from the Berlin NAAFI, and everything, including drinks and smokes, was duty free. There was also a restaurant for lunches only, where we were glad to get a meal at last.

That same evening we were invited to a party. Never before had I seen drink flow so freely. I couldn't help asking how anyone could afford to entertain on so lavish a scale, and was told I'd be doing the same as soon as I got to know the ropes.

As a starter I was advised to get hold of as much coffee as I could, both from the Embassy shop and direct from the UK. I was given the address of a firm which specialised in supplying our Embassies abroad. There was no postage or freight involved: all goods purchased there were delivered straight to the Foreign Office and then sent out in the Diplomatic bag. And everything was tax and duty free.

'If you don't make your pile here, you're a mug.' That's how it was put to me, fair and square. It was black marketing that financed these parties.

'How do I get into the racket?' I asked.

'You get the coffee, and I'll get rid of it for you.'

This helpful colleague got rid of the stuff through an outside contact, and took his own cut in the process. After a while I got fed up with so many middlemen taking their rakeoff, so I tracked down the contact for myself and from then on dealt direct.

Coffee bought at about 35 shillings sold for the equivalent of £40. Lipsticks and other cosmetics, especially with a well-known name such as Coty or Max Factor, were another profitable line. Scotch, gin, brandy and English cigarettes were in demand. Consumer goods were in very short supply: a good line was in gents' natty suitings, Western-style women's clothing, and nylons. A cheap beaver lamb coat could command a fantastic profit.

I was advised by one member of the Embassy staff to send for a Hoover vacuum cleaner. This came free of purchase tax at about £17, and I had no difficulty in selling it for 3,000 szloties, which I exchanged in the Embassy at the staff concession rate of 11.7 szloties to the pound.

The ease with which all this could be done was one of the main reasons why people volunteered to do a tour of duty in Iron Curtain countries. You could save your salary and allowances, live off your takings on the black market, and even save a bit of that as well if you knew how to convert it into the right currency. A lot of tales were told after my trial of the fortunes I made importing penicillin. It's significant that nothing of the kind was even hinted at during the trial itself. I only once did anything about importing drugs into Poland. The child of a British war bride married to a Pole was ill and needed, said their local doctor, streptomycin. I managed by devious means to get my hands on some for them—and didn't take a ha'penny for it.

Diplomatic bags were conveyed to Warsaw by an RAF freighter which, under some clause in the Yalta or Potsdam Agreement, was permitted to land at Warsaw Airport each Wednesday. This was met by Embassy staff with a truck. The flight crew and King's Messenger, later Queen's Messenger, were allowed as a concession as far as the airport refreshment rooms, where they were always given a bottle of vodka and a carton of duty-free English cigarettes, which they would probably be able to get through Customs when returning to England as travellers from abroad.

I never really understood where all the money came from for this widespread black marketing. Poland had been ravaged by the war, but most Poles appeared to be dressed reasonably well—Central European rather than Western fashion, admittedly. I never saw a ragged child, nor anyone who had to go barefoot as some of my friends and relations had done when I was a lad.

Another source of income for the smart operator was the institution known as Commis shops. These were Polish Government shops which for a small commission (hence the name) sold unwanted goods on display at the seller's asking price. I never saw anything cheap in them. Selling through Commis shops wasn't officially frowned on, so it was a simple matter to send home for goods and clothing through the usual channel, put them in the shop, name your own price—and get it. I well remember the wife of one of the Diplomatic staff who asked me to go along with her as she wanted to flog two silver fox furs she'd been given as a wedding present but which she didn't much like. After being on show for a week, these were sold. She made more than twenty times their UK value, and decided she could afford to replace the wedding present. Using one-twentieth of her winnings, she invested in two more furs—but got greedy again, so that they too went to the Commis shop. How many times she repeated the performance, I don't know.

The policy of the higher ranking staff was of course to show horror at the black market exploits of their juniors. They were able to maintain this holier-than-thou attitude while, in many cases, letting their wives do their own deals in this field.

A certain Mrs X came to me one day and asked if I could get rid of a tin of coffee for her without letting her husband know: 'He'd kill me if he knew I was on the Black.' I agreed, and passed it on to my Polish go-between. He paid me with a 500-szloty note, the only one of this denomination I ever saw. At 11.7 to the £ this was pretty valuable, so I marked it with a couple of pinholes in one corner while my go-between made a secret mark of his own, in case at any stage the note rolled back to us as a dud: we'd heard reports of many duds in circulation.

One of my jobs in the Naval Attaché's office was to look after the petty cash. The morning after paying Mrs X her money I had a visit from her husband, enquiring if I could change a 500-szloty note into smaller denominations. When I took the note from him I wasn't all that surprised to find it was the same note I had given his wife the day before. So much for killing her if she went on the Black!

When I was in the dock at the Old Bailey I noticed several former friends gloating there like harpies at the foot of the guillotine, though without their knitting. Mrs X was among them. I wouldn't mind betting she had sticky pants when I was describing my black market activities in Warsaw.

Looking back, I'd say I was neither a big-time operator nor a small-time fiddler. By Embassy standards at the time I reckon I was about par for the course.

In spite of the profits and luxuries available through such methods, there were still many discomforts to be endured. As I've said, I had been posted here to work in the Naval Attaché's office. There were only the two of us on Admiralty staff in the Embassy. A new Attaché arrived ten days after I got there, and I was in fact relieving his predecessor's daughter, who had done the same job for her father and, living with her parents in their quarters, hadn't needed the flat which nominally went with the job. She in her turn had taken over from a civilian whose flat had been leased by the Admiralty at Kwiatowa 9, fully furnished. But when I came to ask for that flat, which was officially mine, there was nothing doing.

While the Naval Attaché's daughter was living with Mum and Dad it had been agreed that the flat could be used by a Scotswoman who had married a Pole during the war and returned with him to Warsaw. When Peggy and I arrived we were dumped not in our appointed place but in a flat belonging to the Foreign Office, in the bare condition I've already described. I made one attempt after another to get our proper accommodation, but without success. The next best thing was to draw some furniture from Embassy stock to make our surroundings bearable. Here again I got a refusal, on the grounds that the Foreign Office didn't supply furniture for Admiralty use. The geyser in the bathroom was broken and wouldn't geyse; the coal range in the kitchen finally packed up; we had always to take our main meal of the day at the Embassy canteen and on Sundays at the Club. Appeals to higher levels went unheeded. They were all right, Jack. In their little cliques, nobody wanted to help anybody else: Air, Naval and Military Attachés all suffered from the same petty rivalries with each other and with the Foreign Office.

Then a British Council flat fell vacant and was offered to us. I went to see it, found it nicely furnished, and decided it was just the thing. We made all our arrangements, and moved in—to find that this, too, had been practically stripped of furniture by the British Council on the familiar grounds that it wasn't up to them to supply the Admiralty with furniture. At least the cooking range functioned; but here again the geyser was useless, and all bath water had to be heated on the range. I never did get my rightful flat or adequate furniture, and even had to buy a dining table locally so that we could have something to eat from. It came home with me in due course, and I still have it.

At home one would have one's Union or Staff Organisation to call on if an agreement was not honoured. Unfortunately I was the only member in Warsaw of my particular Staff Organisation. All I could do was write and complain to headquarters in London. But if I were too frank about what was going on, there was the distinct possibility of my being sent home on some trumped-up excuse and being replaced by a non-Union member who wouldn't give trouble. I decided to leave well alone. I was making so much money on the side that it was worth putting up with sub-standard accommodation.

With the abundance of cash from the activities I've described, and with little else to do but get together with colleagues or go to the Club, there was a party almost every evening in one flat or another. It was at one such that I was introduced to a Polish girl who was to play an important part in my life, not just in Warsaw but quite some time after I'd returned to England.

Chapter Three

Drink and Diplomacy

Karytzia was one of the few who had actually succeeded in escaping from a concentration camp. She still bore the tattooed number above her wrist. There was to be some speculation later about her being a member of the UB, the Polish Secret Police, but to this day I am convinced she wasn't.

Then how had she infiltrated into a party given by a member of the British Embassy staff?

An attractive woman using her wits can get anywhere she wants to go. Karytzia lived in the block of flats where that particular party was being held, and was friendly with our host's wife. She could slip with no great risk between one door and another. An educated woman with a good command of the English language, she made an instant impression on me. We started talking, and went on talking. We met again. I found I wanted to keep on meeting her, and the feeling seemed to be reciprocated. Through her I was able to meet the Polish man in the street, and found him charming.

There was a twitchy feeling at the Embassy that the entire civilian population was made up of potential informers, and we were given instructions to avoid contact with them. This was hammered home so hard to newcomers that for a while one distrusted every Pole on sight. It was a misguided policy. The average Pole was courteous, friendly and hospitable, and I was proud to have several of them as friends.

Such friendships didn't help one's career.

One evening I attended a cocktail party at the Embassy, and when it was over a group of us decided to go on to the flat of Bill Y, one of the Diplomatic Wireless Service Operators. We discovered there wasn't room for all of us in the available cars, so Jack E and myself said we'd find our own way there by tram-car. Naturally we were conversing in English on this tram, and the only other person on it, a woman of about forty years of age, suddenly said in excellent, cultivated English how marvellous it was to hear people speaking in her own language once more. She obviously came from a good family, mentioned that she'd been to Girton—and there was no reason to disbelieve her. Like many others, she had met and married a Polish officer during the war and come here to live.

We reached our stop. Her destination was further on but we invited her to get off and come for a drink with us, to meet a few more English people. She gladly accepted, and during the short walk to the flat explained how she and her husband had tried to settle down here after the war. When Poland became Communist, those who had fought alongside the Western Allies rather than with the Russians found themselves in disfavour, and her husband lost his position. He was now a school caretaker, and she earned a little by teaching English at evening classes.

When we arrived at the flat the poor woman, who had been so much looking forward to this interlude, got a very cold reception from some of the folk there. It was so marked that some of the more sympathetic guests apologised to her for the behaviour of the others. Anyhow, when she left we saw to it that she took with her some delicacies, brought here from the Embassy canteen, which were unobtainable elsewhere in Poland.

The next day we found that our own UB had been at work. In England we pride ourselves that we don't have a Secret Police force, but what else are Special Branch or the Security Service, MI5 and MI6? It would surprise many people if they really knew the identity of those strangers with whom they find themselves in conversation in our hotels, pubs and elsewhere. And, as in the Secret Police of other nations, there are plenty of them swollen with power, anxious to 'fix' suspects and to work off their strange psychological perversities.

They are well represented in our Diplomatic services and other delegations abroad. Our own little lot were waiting to accuse us that morning after the party. Someone in the flat had reported our misdemeanour, and both Jack and I received a reprimand for entertaining a local.

'She might have been a UB plant,' we were told.

How frightened can people get? We ourselves didn't even know we'd be travelling by tram-car until the last minute, and couldn't have predicted the time the tram would come along. The woman was already a passenger, on her way home, when we boarded it. She was as English as could be. Of course this didn't necessarily prevent her being a member of the UB, but even their most skilled operatives could hardly have been that psychic. If anyone could have seen the expression of pure joy on the poor woman's face when she heard us speaking her native tongue, they'd have known then and there that she was genuine.

There was one young Polish lady who had no trouble in being accepted at parties. She was assistant to the Embassy doctor, and was known to all of us as Doctor Betty. She had all the warmth and fire of her Slavonic race. I imagine she was harried by the UB and urged to gossip about what she saw and heard, but I doubt whether they ever got anything out of her: she was no more a menace to us than our visitor from the tram-car had been.

Things with Peggy continued to deteriorate. She hankered to see her daughter again, didn't like the conditions under which we were living in Warsaw, and after a spell of leave decided she'd rather stay in England than return to Poland.

I must confess this didn't hurt me too acutely. Karytzia could come to visit me more often. As a sign that there was no-one in the flat but myself I would place a lighted reading lamp in the window, visible from the street. Going to visit Poles in their homes, as I frequently did, would have been a serious matter for me if it had been known at the Embassy. It would have been regarded as equally serious to entertain a Pole, particularly an attractive Polish girl, in my own quarters.

From their side, I imagine the Polish authorities were well aware of our clandestine meetings. The block of flats in which I lived on Aleja Jerosolimski had no direct entrance from the street. The only way in was through a gate leading to the courtyard and then up the stairs to the flats. The gate was always locked after dark. To enter or leave, one had to ring for the *dzorza*, in this case a pleasant, smart young man who spent hours drinking my whisky while trying to teach me the Polish language. Pleasant he may have been, but my flat was a foreigner's and it was part of his job to report my movements. The fact that I was entertaining a Polish visitor could hardly have been overlooked. Officially it was no crime for Poles to visit foreigners, but such a state of tension existed between East and West that they on their side were just as ready as our own people to view such meetings as near-criminal.

Mind you, they might have had grounds for disapproval if they had realised that by now Karytzia had set herself up as my chief black market agent. A skilled and persuasive interpreter, she was able to deal most competently on my behalf. There were fixed rates for tea, coffee and cigarettes, but such items as clothing, shoes, medical preparations, branded electrical goods and so on were always subject to hard bargaining. At that time the only nail varnish to be obtained in Poland was scarlet, and of poor quality, so we were able to do a brisk trade in various other shades obtainable from the UK.

Karytzia would rarely accept a great deal for her help, but was grateful for Max Factor lipsticks or Coty face powder now and again.

On one occasion she saved me from being murdered.

I had sent to England for a cheap beaver lamb coat, and arranged to meet a prospective buyer at a rendezvous in the rubble of what had once been the Warsaw ghetto. We went to the ghetto area in an old Anglia car I had at that time, and I had with me a gun which I had taken, on Karytzia's advice, from the office: there were several left over from the time when the Germans had used the place during the war. I did my business with the buyer of the fur coat and was picking my way back through the rubble towards the car when two shots rang out and I heard a groan behind me. Apparently a second man, whether in league with the buyer or not I don't know, was about to pounce on me from the back with a knife in his hand, presumably for the cash I had in my possession. Karytzia had kept back in the shadows, keeping the buyer covered with my gun in case of any funny business, and it was sheer good fortune that my assailant hadn't known she was there.

We didn't wait to check whether the man was dead or not. *I* certainly would have been dead if I'd got that knife in my back. It took us very little time to get to the car and dash home for a large noggin of Scotch. On all future occasions when we did business with strangers in secluded spots we went armed.

Weekends were the time when the Club established by members of the Western bloc was at its busiest. You found British, Americans, French and Scandinavians there, plus all sorts of miscellaneous bods who turned up from time to time, about whom it was the rule not to ask too many questions. Quite apart from members of Western Embassies and Missions, and such agencies as the British Council and Passport Control, there were personnel of British construction companies erecting factories in Poland, and other businessmen passing through, so that half the time one didn't know whom one was speaking to.

I was anxious to buy a car that a Frenchman had for sale, and as he would accept only American dollars in payment, I let it be known at the Club that I was willing to pay over the odds in szloties for dollars. It wasn't long before I was accosted at the bar one Sunday lunchtime by a perfect stranger speaking in what sounded to me like an American accent. He asked if I was the person interested in getting his hands on some American currency, and when I said this was so he suggested we drink up and take a stroll along the bank of the Vistula, which flowed past the bottom of the Club grounds.

We sat down and watched a skein of wild geese pass overhead, and after some casual conversation he asked if I was willing to *earn* some dollars. When I displayed interest he swore me to secrecy before going on to make a proposition. Then he warned me that there was an element of danger if anything went wrong, and if I was caught I'd have to face up to things alone: no-one from the West would want to know.

I suppose I ought to have beaten a hasty retreat right then, but I was intrigued, and asked what he wanted me to do.

He promised 300 dollars for each time I followed certain instructions. These were to drive to a given spot outside the capital and deposit a small package. The first was to be left off a forest track by the Modlin road: he named the exact place where I was to turn off the road and hide the car in a clearing, and gave explicit orders for hiding the package itself. There was rarely a great deal of traffic on the road other than the odd car and an occasional horse-drawn wagon, but if I had the slightest suspicion that anyone was following I was to drive on and not leave the package.

Every foreign resident who owned a car in Poland was issued with number plates giving the registration numbers in yellow on a black background instead of the usual white on black—presumably for the benefit of the police and the UB. Also, every road out of the city had a police check point where all cars had to stop and produce registration documents and personal documents. If the occupants of a car with yellow number plates held medium or high diplomatic rank, or were Service Attachés in Western Embassies, this car would be held up on some pretext or other for a short time before being allowed to proceed, during which time the checkpoint police would whistle up a UB Citroen to tail the car diligently until it returned to the city. Some were followed for days on end when Attachés went touring the country. Junior staff was rarely subjected to this tailing procedure, which was probably why this American had approached me.

Even so, there was always a danger of the package, whatever it was, being discovered at the check point. I stressed this to Al, as he'd told me to call him, and said that if I had to run such risks I wasn't going to take less than 500 dollars a trip. To this he eventually agreed.

The packages were always brought to my flat by Al in person, and were so well wrapped and sealed that I never did discover what the contents were. I was very curious. Invariably there was a smaller sealed packet to be brought back, which I suspect contained the venue for the next collection. I made several trips at about fortnightly or three-weekly intervals, and soon amassed the necessary dollars to buy the car from the Frenchman. The trips were entirely uneventful until the last one.

I was about to place the package in a hole beneath a boulder some ten paces in from a kilometre stone when, to my horror, instead of the expected small packet for return I found a human hand cut off at the wrist. There was only one thing to do: to get the hell out of it as quickly as possible. I got moving, but was conscious that I still had with me the package that ought to have been left at the boulder. I had driven out with it blithely enough, but somehow the thought of passing in through the check point with it gave me the jitters. I preferred to get rid of it as quickly as possible. A few yards on from a bridge crossing a fast-flowing stream I stopped the car, put the package into a string bag I had in the car for shopping, weighted it with stones, and dropped it into the water. I got back into Warsaw without incident, though I don't mind admitting that every time I saw a car behind me I thought it was the UB catching up. Even after all this time I can't understand why a day and night watch wasn't kept at that last rendezvous to catch the person who would sooner or later show up there.

When Al arrived at the flat he was furious that I'd ditched his package.

'Did you open it?'

'I was in too much of a hurry to get rid of the blasted thing,' I assured him. 'I wasn't going to waste time seeing what it was.'

He took some persuading, and made it clear that if my story was true—which it was—I should have stuck my neck out by bringing the hot material back in again in my car. I reminded him of what he'd told me during our talk beside the Vistula: if I'd been caught I'd have had to face up to things alone...so it was up to me *not* to get caught with anything in the car.

I never saw Al again. I conjectured that those packages contained payment or instructions, or both, for foreign spies working in Poland—or maybe for Poles spying for the West. Could Al have been a member of the CIA? Or was there some other Western agency supporting subversive activities against the Polish State? Could the organisation have cracked up; or could one of them have proved a danger and been eliminated, the human hand being placed there as a sign to Al that it was too dangerous to continue? It was a pretty gruesome way of conveying a message.

Karytzia was very angry when I told her about my exploits on Al's behalf. I got round to doing this weeks later, when it was clear Al wasn't going to show up again and I no longer considered myself bound to secrecy—not as far as Karytzia was concerned, anyway. When she had calmed down she remembered that just after the period I had been describing to her she had read in the newspaper *Trybuni Ludi* that because of discord in a group of what she called partisans—dissidents on the run from the Communist regime —the authorities had discovered one of their hideouts in the forest. It had been raided: several were killed, others arrested. In getting mixed up with Al I had exposed not only myself but her to danger, since if I'd been picked up she would undoubtedly have been suspect herself and would probably have been arrested.

The Club, where Al had first approached me, had many functions. It was a great place for discussing scandal—and for making it. In the constricted life we led, a certain amount of illicit love-making and wife-swapping was inevitable. It was amusing to see some of the pillars of respectability studiously ignoring their lovers while in the presence of their wives or husbands.

An attaché at a certain Embassy was reputed to be having a violent love affair with an Ambassador's secretary. No-one thought his sweet little wife was aware of this until, one Sunday afternoon during the summer when the veranda of the Club was packed with people having tea or stronger drinks, a terrific fight broke out between the two women. Hair was pulled, there was a lot of punching and scratching, and one even pulled off her shoe and pounded the other with her stiletto heel until they were separated. The poor deceived wife wasn't seen at the Club again, but returned to her own country, while lover girl brazened it out and continued in her job as Ambassador's secretary.

In our own Embassy I once had occasion to stay a bit late during the lunch break, and had to go to a certain office for a reference book. I tapped on the door but walked straight in, not expecting anyone to be there at that particular time. To my amazement I saw, stretched out on the richly carpeted floor, a high-ranking Embassy official *sans* trousers and jacket, copulating like a buck rabbit with another official's secretary-typist. I excused myself and departed. In his eagerness to get down to things, the silly man had omitted the elementary precaution of locking his office door.

At one Embassy there was a very eligible, good-looking and reputedly well-to-do bachelor whose friendship was cultivated by many of the women, the single ones with a view to matrimony and the married ones for other reasons. They were all disappointed by his refusal to nibble at the bait. Little did they know he was a homosexual: he certainly showed no outward signs of it. I wouldn't have guessed it myself if I hadn't accepted an invitation to his place for a drink one evening and received an unmistakable overture from him. He probably had the idea that as an ex-sailor I must have been in the habit of indulging in the old Naval sport and pastime. I assured him I was doing very happily with the normal thing, thank you, and we parted with no reproaches on either side.

There was a Middle East diplomat who frequently used the Club. As a Moslem he wouldn't touch alcohol but sat contentedly at the bar with a soft drink—a quiet, friendly type. As I got to know him better, the subject of sex came inevitably into our conversation, and when he decided I was a broadminded type he invited me to his flat for what is nowadays called a love-in. These parties were confined to members of Embassy and Mission staffs, plus a small number of selected Polish women and boys.

Not knowing what to expect, I was a bit taken aback to find on entering that the males were directed to one room and the females to another, where they were expected to divest themselves of every article of clothing, except that the women were allowed to retain their handbags. Then, as naked as Adam and Eve, the guests were received by their host in the same state. I will draw a veil over what went on afterwards.

Many people participated in these orgies from time to time, yet they were never discussed outside the flat even amongst those who attended. Although the diplomat had regarded me as a broadminded type, I'm afraid I wasn't broadminded enough to go there again.

It has been widely reported that I was sent home from Warsaw for drinking heavily. I think I can say, as I said about the black market, that I was about average.

At that very first party after arrival in Warsaw, I remember a character who, holding a very responsible and sensitive position, privy to everything that was sent and received and with cipher and decoding matters at his fingertips, decided he would like to have a quarrel with his wife. I found out later that she was accustomed to this when he was in drink, and refused to play. Thwarted, he just stretched out on the floor in a drunken stupor and went to sleep, the guests having either to step over or walk round him. His antics in drink were a byword, but I don't recall that he was sent home as a result.

The Polish Army gave a reception at the Military Academy in honour of Red Army Day, and among the invitations sent out was a batch to the British Embassy. Out of several who attended, three got so pickled on vodka that when they tottered out into the fresh air they fell the full length of the steps leading from the Academy building and lay on the ground until dragged to their cars by their chauffeurs. Their faces were so cut, grazed and bleeding, and their clothing so mangled at knees and elbows, that none of them showed up for work for about two weeks, until the scars had healed. This display by foreign guests of the Polish Army was photographed by the press outside, and there's little doubt that the pictures are now in the Kremlin archives. Many months later in London I was shown prints of these photographs. The trio claimed they had been doped. No one conversant with the gallant traditions of the Polish Army could seriously believe they would put Mickey Finns in the drinks of their invited guests.

In spite of this public display of drunkenness, the three remained at their posts and were not sent home.

A third incident I recall is of a chap who went to what was then about the only night club in Warsaw. He had a drop too much and slept it off on a bench in a nearby park. When he blearily came round it was to find that his watch and wallet were missing. Unknown to him, whilst he was flat out the militiaman on that beat, who knew him by sight, had relieved him of them to prevent anyone stealing them. As the militiaman had to pass the Embassy, he delivered the watch and wallet into safe keeping there. The Ambassador knew everything, yet no action was taken to return this individual to England.

It was some of those self-same people who had the audacity to spread rumours that I was sent home for drunkenness.

Just to set the record straight, when I did get home from Warsaw and reported to the late Mr H. V. Pennells, Civil Assistant to the Director of Naval Intelligence, he told me personally that I had been withdrawn only because of one of those periodical economic crises which so regularly afflict the country and its servants. The Chancellor of the Exchequer, at that time Mr R. A. Butler, had ordered a drastic cut in expenditure, and I was one of those under the chopper. My job was regraded for a single girl, whose allowances would be considerably less than those paid in my case. It was as simple as that.

But I wasn't to worry. 'We've got an appointment for you at Portland.'

Having previously been working at Portsmouth, I thought I'd misheard this. 'You mean Portsmouth?'

'No. Portland.'

Instead of returning to my old duties, as I'd half expected to do, I was sent to what was then the Underwater Detection Establishment, later the Admiralty Underwater Weapons Establishment. If I'd been sent home in disgrace, it was an odd thing for Security-minded authorities to give me an appointment of this kind!

From everybody's point of view it was a fateful posting.

Chapter Four

Recruited

Portland isn't quite an island, being joined to the English mainland by a causeway under Chesil beach which can be covered with water at times and is all too often scoured by treacherous cross-winds; but in essence it is well and truly insular. Long before the Navy brought its secret research teams here it was by nature secretive, dour and self-centred.

The quarries dug out of the great mass of limestone have breathed up an off-white dust which lies over everything, and the local stone used in so many houses makes even a small villa look like a hostile fortress.

Looking down into one quarry, a visitor is reported to have said: 'You could put St Paul's Cathedral in there.'

'St Paul's Cathedral came out of there,' was the truthful response.

Within living memory a Portland man who brought a wife home from the mainland was, in company with his unfortunate choice, stoned off this Dorset Gibraltar. Seeing an apparent stranger, the local's first suspicious query is: 'Is 'e one o' we?' The development of the Naval Base has made a slight dent in this; but, being clannish in itself, only a dent and not a breakthrough. Portland stone is pretty solid.

Yet there's something fascinating about it. Even those with grim memories of it—and since it once had a prison which is now a bleak Borstal, there are plenty of them—often come back to wander round and marvel at their memories.

I started work at UDE, the Underwater Detection Establishment, in November 1952, and was there until January 1957, when I was transferred to the Port Auxiliary Repair Unit. After early 1960 I was the sole clerical officer in the unit, responsible for acceptance, distribution and filing of all papers pertaining to the unit.

Karytzia was distraught when she heard the news of my departure from Warsaw. I was pretty confused myself. There was nothing we could do; no time in which to sort things out. If Peggy and I had definitely parted by then, if there'd been a divorce and Karytzia

26

could have married me, she would undoubtedly have done so, become a British citizen, and come home to the UK with me. At least, that's how we would have tried to organise things. Even without Peggy, there would have been some very jagged obstacles to clear. We wouldn't have been allowed to marry while I was employed in the Embassy, and once I was back in England the chances of my getting a visa for a personal return visit were small. Karytzia's chances of getting one to come and see me in England were even smaller.

I found a small cottage on the outskirts of Weymouth, within easy distance of my job on Portland, and here Peggy and I made an attempt to pick up our married life again. It didn't show any signs of picking up, I'm afraid. Her daughter Margaret's husband was a serviceman, and they had married quarters in Portsmouth. Peggy liked to spend most of her time with them. I saw very little of her, and as well as settling into my new job found that I had to do most of my own cooking and housework.

Karytzia and I corresponded regularly at first. Her letters came to an accommodation address, in order not to make things more difficult with Peggy. I sent small parcels of cosmetics and nylons when I could get them. We went on writing, but it all began to seem a bit unreal.

And then on the Base I met, in a neighbouring office, Ethel Gee. Or, rather, we renewed an acquaintanceship which she had forgotten but I hadn't.

One of the few truthful things the newspapers have ever reported about me was my saying that Bunty—as Ethel has always been known to her friends—was a woman in a million. It's true: true that I said it, and true that she is. Even during those awful years in prison she never once reproached me for deceiving her and getting her into this terrible situation, though she had every reason for doing so. Because I conned her: it's the only word for it. She suffered unjustly because of me.

But in those early days at Portland we had no idea that the prison shadows would ever reach out towards us.

Bunty had nothing whatsoever to do with the break-up of my marriage. It had been a marriage in name only for a long time; I saw Peggy less and less.

My friendship with Bunty began casually enough with my reminding her that we had met when I was visiting people I knew in

Gosport during the war. As time went on, this friendship deepened and in my case turned into love. Bunty, however, kept me at arm's length because she knew I was a married man. She was shy about even accepting a lift in my car if I met her on the way to the office in the mornings, but finally agreed to do this, and eventually I made a practice of dropping her off on the way home also.

I sensed that my feelings were being reciprocated, though she still kept her distance until at last I told her the truth about my matrimonial position. She viewed this with some scepticism at the start.

'I've heard everything now,' I can hear her saying. 'That knocks spots off the "My wife doesn't understand me" yarn.'

Gradually she came to believe me, and although she was still shy and self-conscious about it she consented to go out with me occasionally.

Bunty was first employed at the Underwater Detection Establishment in October 1950. She became an established civil servant in January 1957 and was employed as such at the Establishment from then on. She worked in Stores section up to 1955, and then went into the Drawing Office Record section.

Stories have been told of lavish weekends we spent in London together. In fact, getting Bunty away for even one innocent day unchaperoned was quite a feat. Sharing her Portland home were her ageing mother, aunt and uncle, all of whom she looked after and most of whose rigid standards she had been brought up to accept. The idea that she could gad off to London for carefree weekends whenever she chose is ridiculous.

Besides, I was hardly in a position to throw money around. It was true that I had some stacked away—but I had no intention of drawing attention to this, and never gave even Bunty a hint of its existence.

It had come with me from Warsaw. When I was preparing to leave, I had to decide what to do with the profits I had accumulated from the black market. If I tried to convert them into English currency through official channels, a lot of questions would be asked; and if I then paid the lot into my bank, both Exchange control and the Inland Revenue would also ask some sticky questions. Instead, I got one of my contacts to convert my szloties into American dollars at a fantastic rate of exchange. The dollar was then the currency everybody wanted. English money wasn't much respected: English lipsticks, I'm afraid, rated higher than pound notes. This being so, there were plenty of people willing to sell English currency for dollars. Anyone who wanted to escape the country—and there was many a Pole anxious to quit—needed dollars to bribe his way out. I got a good rate for mine, and smuggled the resulting English money out without too many heart-flutterings.

As I've said, I wasn't going to throw this around too lavishly once I was home.

After a while Karytzia's letters ceased. I thought perhaps she had found someone else. She had often said she longed to go to America: maybe she'd managed that in the end, and had forgotten all about me. I could hardly blame her, since there didn't seem to be much future for the two of us when we were so far apart.

There was another possibility which I didn't like to think of. Unfortunately it was the likeliest one. She could be in trouble for writing letters to the West and receiving them in return.

One afternoon the phone rang in my office. My caller gave no name but said he had recently come from Poland and had a message from Karytzia.

I didn't know what to think. Was it a genuine message: did she still live in hope, or was she in real trouble?

He asked if I could meet him in London.

I agreed to go up the next Saturday or Sunday. He favoured the Sunday, and of all places to meet suggested Dulwich Art Gallery.

That was where it all started.

In my trial I admit I told some pretty lurid stories. When you're fighting for your freedom against a massive opposition with all the advantages on its side, you can't afford to stick too scrupulously to accurate details. The dice are loaded. Until you're there in the dock, you don't realise just how loaded. When the denunciations chucked at you are based on largely unreliable, cunningly slanted testimony, and in some cases flagrant misrepresentation, you're surely entitled to fight them back with their own weapons. I did quite a bit of colourful embroidery. It didn't do me much good: but the simple unvarnished truth wouldn't have served me much better.

I told the judge and jury about that first meeting in Dulwich. The man waiting for me was a complete stranger. In my version in Court I used the name 'Christina' for the girl, still hoping to protect her—if she wasn't by now utterly beyond protection. She had been only a bait to lure me to the meeting, and now we got down to reality: what the Poles wanted was information from Portland Naval Base. I refused to give it, and was told that things could be made rough not only for me but for my wife and Bunty. At last I agreed to meet this man later, on a prearranged date, at the Toby Jug on Kingston by-pass; but when I showed up there I handed over only some bits and pieces copied from local newspapers.

They weren't satisfied. Threats were redoubled. When I tried to fob them off with further useless material, they sent two thugs down to give me a terrific beating in the caravan where I was by now living. When I failed to attend a meeting to which I'd been summoned, I got another violent going-over. I was reminded of how the Russians had succeeded in getting Trotsky in the end, and was told that the life of Petrov, who had defected in a blaze of publicity in Australia, was now not worth living: fear had driven him into raging alcoholism.

That's the way I told it, with a lot of dramatic embellishments.

And just one part of it was true. The whole thing really did begin, that day, with Karytzia.

There was no doubt in my mind that, given the chance, she'd get clear of Poland. The man I met outside the Art Gallery confirmed this. To this day I don't know his name: he soon bowed out, and it became clear that I was in the hands of the Russians and not of the Poles who had established the contact. He made it clear, anyway, that they knew all it was necessary to know about the two of us, and that Karytzia would indeed like to leave. She wasn't happy in her homeland. 'Politically unreliable' was the phrase he used about her. There was nevertheless the implication that, deplorably unreliable and unpatriotic as she might be, they'd be prepared to consider some kind of leniency towards her—might make a deal—if I would play along with them.

Playing along meant supplying them with information from Portland Naval Base.

I said I wasn't going to get involved in anything of that kind. In which case, he said, *they* could make things very unpleasant for Karytzia. *They* had their methods. I was still keen on her, wasn't I? I wouldn't want her to suffer, would I? If I wanted her to be set free, to go where she wanted to go, to come to me if that was what both of us wanted, then I knew what to do. *They* could arrange things—one way or the other.

It was up to me.

It's easy enough to say I ought to have gone straight to the police or reported to my superiors. Also easy enough to say that, even if I felt justified in going along with them a little way, I ought to have demanded some cast-iron guarantee that Karytzia would be sent over before I took another step. When it comes to the crunch and you're facing such a situation personally, how easy do you find it to make a calm, rational appraisal?

I'm the one who went through all this. I'm the one who knows just how difficult it is to make a straight deal and to decide how far it's safe to go, only to find out too late that it's just that—*too late*.

Putting it bluntly, all the later mistakes stemmed from that first mistake—chasing a bit of skirt behind the Iron Curtain. If I'd had any sense I'd have put all memories of her well behind me. But I still felt a vague responsibility for her. There ought to be some way of getting her out and letting her lead her own life, where she wanted to lead it, the way she wanted to lead it. I hoped that by stringing these folk along I could get her a visa as a *quid pro quo*. By the time I was hopelessly compromised I learned that this wouldn't be countenanced. The Russians weren't interested in Karytzia as a person or in my feelings for her, except insofar as these improved her effectiveness as bait. Once I was hooked, it was too late to wish I hadn't bitten so gullibly. They drew me in— sometimes slowly, sometimes with a cruel tug—until I was well in the net. By the time I realised that the bait of half-threats and half-promises about Karytzia was just pie in the sky, I was too deeply enmeshed to struggle free. Demands made on me grew more and more intense: I had to cope with these, with my everyday routine, and with my deepening feelings for Bunty.

One of my first contacts was a Russian always referred to as Nikki. He was not the most inconspicuous person I have ever met. He favoured the Russian fashion of a long overcoat with padded shoulders, and invariably wore wide trousers and a broad-brimmed trilby. In fact with his flat face and big ears he was the cartoonist's dream of a Soviet spy. Later he was to be superseded by Gordon Lonsdale.

For the work I was expected to do on the Base I was given a Minox camera which fitted snugly into my pocket. It was about $3\frac{1}{2}''$ long, $1\frac{1}{8}''$ wide, and about $\frac{5}{8}''$ thick, and would easily pass as a cigarette lighter at a glance. It was in fact so unobtrusive that it was never discovered when I was arrested. Anything which couldn't be removed from the Establishment could be photographed with this— by which I mean objects, but not documents, which didn't come out so well. For finer work I had an Exacta camera, which took good pictures of anything I could carry off home with me in the evening.

I was summoned to meetings in various ways, usually by advertising matter in the post. A card from the Scotch House wool shop in Knightsbridge had a certain meaning, as did a brochure about Hoover products. If I received an envelope containing advertising matter about the Sun Life Assurance Company, this meant I was to go to a certain lay-by on the road to Salisbury at exactly 8-pm the night after I received it. The GPO was a lot more reliable then: under present conditions I can't imagine how we'd have operated! If the contact wasn't made, I was to return at the same time on subsequent evenings.

On one occasion I arrived and was asked by my contact, this time the man I came to know as Roman, if there was any means of knowing when HM ships were due to arrive at Portland and when they would depart. This was an easy one. Every day there is issued what's called the Daily State, giving berths of ships and dates of expected arrivals and departures. Roman was disappointed that only 'am' or 'pm' was given, and not the approximate times. Nevertheless I was instructed to get the Daily State for him regularly, though often by the time I was able to pass it on the details were hopelessly out of date.

Then he wanted to know how much I could tell him about the Army artillery ranges at Lulworth. I had to disappoint him. But when we got down to it, it turned out he merely wished to discover if there was any means of checking when the Army would be firing out to seaward. He was taken aback when I told him that such details always appeared in the local press to warn fishermen and were also published in the local Notices to Mariners, which anyone could buy.

On another occasion I was asked what information was available about areas allocated for HM ships to exercise in and the times of such exercises. As with the Daily State, this presented no problems. Each week a programme was issued for the ensuing week specifying ships taking part, together with the place, nature and time of the exercises. Most departments had plenty of copies knocking about, so Roman was placed on the distribution list. If a spare copy couldn't be obtained, I had to make a photographic copy for him.

As parts of this narrative will show, my contacts could never get used to the idea of military information of any kind being available to the general public, or to its being discussed by local inhabitants without fear of immediate imprisonment or banishment to a labour camp.

There can be no doubt whatsoever that the head of our particular group was the man I have referred to as Roman.

Unlike Nikki, Roman dressed quietly and well. He spoke fluent English and could be distinguished as a foreigner only occasionally by the way he gesticulated with his hands during a conversation. Some Englishmen have this mannerism, but in a way peculiar to their breed—Cockneys, for example. Roman's gestures were in the Continental fashion.

I have described one meeting of the group at a lakeside. There were others—other meetings, other faces. I recall a travelling 'inspector' whom I met only in Eire, probably co-ordinating the various groups working in the United Kingdom. The Krogers, who supplied the communication link between England and the Soviet Union for all groups in the field, I didn't meet until it was all over. Another person with whom I had dealings was a nondescript character in the Bunch of Grapes in Kensington—of which more later.

There were at least three others whose functions I can't explain. I had arranged to meet one of the group one Saturday evening at a spot pinpointed on a road map off the A3 near the Marquis of Granby roundabout outside Esher. I was there a minute or two early, and saw my contact being driven past the rendezvous in a car containing two strangers. They could have been there to watch for a police trap or perhaps to have me pointed out to them in case they themselves were needed as go-betweens at a later date. When I asked who they were I was curtly told they were friends out for an evening drive. It was useless to pursue the matter: I ought to have known better than to ask.

The third man to puzzle me was one I met face to face quite a few times, but with whom I never exchanged more than the prearranged recognition sentence. The moment we had transacted our business he departed immediately. He seemed to have no direct liaison with the others, yet they knew of him and I've even been given small packages to pass on to him. It was almost as though I'd been casually appointed as go-between. Maybe he was a courier between our group and another, or maybe between several groups. One thing is clear: as I was an amateur, nothing other than what directly concerned me would ever be disclosed about the others involved.

I've just described myself as an amateur. It's inconceivable that all these people were in England solely to deal with the scraps of information I might be able to supply. The GRU and KGB wouldn't have wasted all that manpower for something so speculative. After all, when they approached me they couldn't be sure I was going to be of any value to them. They would hardly have built up such a complex network on the off-chance. And when I did begin to work for them, showing up on average once a month and rarely supplying more than a few items at a time...no, it was too expensive an investment for what they got out of me or could ever hope to get out of me. Roman was obviously supervising a lot of other people, engaged on a lot of other things.

I have had two Renault cars, the first being one of the old 750-cc rear-engine jobs, which I traded in for a new Renault Dauphine. I was given instructions that any time I received literature through the post about Renault cars, such as a brochure about new models, I was to hold it up to the light and examine it thoroughly. If there was a pin-hole through the centre I was to go into the gents' lavatory at Alresford on my next trip to London at 2-pm precisely.

There were two WCs inside this public convenience. Going in at 2-pm on the dot, I was to enter the one on my left, take out a package which I would find behind the door, put it in my pocket and proceed to London. This package, never much larger than a flat 2-oz. tobacco tin, was always sealed with sellotape and I was never able to satisfy my curiosity about it.

Whoever selected this pick-up point did so with total disregard for my nerves: the lavatory was in a cul-de-sac slap-bang opposite Alresford Police Station.

Anyone knowing the time of my arrival could deposit the package, taking his cue from the sound of the Renault coming up the 200-yard approach, and leave by a footpath which led off I don't know where, without my seeing him. On one corner was a hotel, its gardens and stables behind a wall on one side of the street. On the other corner was a cycle shop, and next to it a cinema where a kids' programme had usually started by the time I passed.

What bewildered me, and still does, is why a sleepy little place like Alresford should have been chosen and what there was in the vicinity which could have interested the Russians. Of course Portsmouth, Southampton and Salisbury Plain are within easy motoring distance, which made it as good a spot as any.

Having obtained the package, it was my routine to proceed to a rendezvous near London and meet whoever might show up there, to get any instructions on other matters before I went on into Kensington. Once or twice I mentioned that I had a package from Alresford with me, and each time got a dour brush-off on the lines of, 'So, you know your instructions what to do with it.'

What I had to do with it was go to the Bunch of Grapes public house in Brompton Road at a given time and stand by a door at the rear of the bar leading into the gents' toilet. (They seem to have had a fixation on lavatories for this part of the operation!) I was to hold a newspaper in my left hand. I probably had a drink in the other. A man would approach and say:

'Is that the evening paper you've got there?'

'No, I'm afraid it's a daily.'

'I wanted the racing results.'

I've often wondered what would have happened if some genuine enquirer had really wanted the racing results.

Contact made, my questioner would disappear into the gents', and after a brief interval I would follow and hand him the package. He then vanished from the scene. We met several times like this, and each time observed the same ritual although we had come to know each other by sight. He was a shabby, nondescript individual, a little taller than myself, very thin and looking as though a good meal would do him good. Usually he seemed in need of a shave, and wore a shiny navy blue suit and, on the last occasion we met, a tight-fitting navy blue overcoat obviously not made for him.

Not all these assignations were made in London. First Nikki and then others would come to see me at Weymouth; a procedure with some snags, and some advantages.

While all this had been going on I was still trying to sort out the turmoil of my private life. The fresh starts which Peggy and I had attempted from time to time never lasted more than a couple of days. She spent more and more time in Portsmouth, and at last I told her I wasn't prepared to go on like this. Rather than take action on my own, on the grounds that our marriage had never been valid in the first place, I agreed not to defend a divorce action which she brought on grounds of cruelty. While this was going through—it took quite a time—I allowed Peggy to have the house when she needed it, and I moved out.

I bought myself a caravan.

This proved most useful. I found a pleasant site in the country some miles outside Weymouth and lived alone there for many months, travelling daily to and from work at Portland Naval Base. Anyone who wanted to come and see me could do so with little fear of being disturbed by unannounced visitors. I think my contacts rather relished the chance of a day out in the country, and for myself I was able to cut out a lot of that trailing to and from London. Quite apart from the time, expense and possible risks involved, those London trips were becoming hard to explain to Bunty, whom I was now taking out most weekends.

One great drawback was the lack of electricity on the site, making it virtually impossible for me to photograph documents at home with the Exacta.

I would have to find somewhere else, with a suitable power supply.

I searched the whole area and could find nowhere that fitted in with all our requirements. Then one afternoon Nikki was with me on Portland, photographing some radar installations (since dismantled), and during our wanderings we noticed some holiday caravans in the grounds of a club. We did a covert recce and discovered that the toilets on the site had electric lights. This, we decided, was the place for me: it would be simple to run a cable from the toilets to the caravan.

Then we found that the site was licensed for the summer months only. I made a few enquiries and learned that I could happily be accommodated during the rest of the year as well: the site operators were heavily involved financially with the owners of the land, and were only too pleased to have a little something coming in during the close season.

I asked if I could rent an electricity meter and connect my caravan to the mains supply. Permission was readily granted, so I was now able to photograph any of my borrowings in the seclusion of the caravan.

Eventually quite a few other people followed my example and came to live on the site, some of them with sensitive Naval jobs in other establishments on the Isle of Portland. I made friends with a few, and at no time did I attempt to extract any information from them, nor did any scrap of information come involuntarily from them that I made use of. If any of them should read what follows, they have my full assurance on this matter: our friendship and conversation there were quite separate from the clandestine side of my life.

Whatever differences there may be between us nowadays, I'm sure they would need no persuasion to agree with me on one thing:

the caravan site, on a cliff-top some 600-ft above sea level, was one of the draughtiest places in the British Isles.

One evening in my car, on the outskirts of London, Roman produced some Admiralty charts of Portland and its approaches—freely obtainable from the Hydrographical Department's agents and in no way secret—and asked me to pinpoint exactly where my caravan was sited. (Actually, he used the word 'stationed'.) I did this and thought no more about it: they always wanted everything checked down to the last little detail, and I remember that earlier they had even wanted a scale drawing of my Weymouth cottage, both inside and outside.

Anyway, they certainly knew how to get there by the time they had finished. They soon discovered, as I'd discovered for myself, the disadvantages.

One can live in a great city unaware of one's neighbours and unobserved by them. In the small community where I had now settled, the neighbours made it their business to know as much as possible about those invading their rock. They mentally registered the comings and goings of all callers, whether tradesmen or personal acquaintances. I pointed out that it was unwise to have people they couldn't account for rolling up too often, and we then struck a balance between visits to me on the caravan site and trips by me to London.

At one Saturday meeting near Worcester Park station, Nikki suggested that as he had a table booked at the Mirabelle that evening I should accompany him to meet a friend. I was only too happy to do so, but commented that it wasn't a very good idea for him to carry the incriminating films, drawings and documents I had just handed over to him. He had already thought of this and was arranging to get rid of them: he'd meet me, he said, in the Haymarket at nine that evening. This gave me nice time to get to my hotel, clean up, and cancel a previous tentative arrangement I'd made.

We duly met, and made our way through the Saturday evening crowds to the restaurant. I wondered who the friend was that he proposed to introduce to me.

A table had been reserved. As we sat down I saw that it was laid for four. I was about to observe that he'd mentioned my meeting only one other person, when a smartly dressed couple arrived at the table and were introduced as John and his wife. Nikki said

I was to have a good look at John, as I'd be seeing him quite a lot in the future. This proved to be correct.

Nikki's padded shoulders and wide Oxford bags made quite a contrast to John's soberly cut London suit. They were poles apart. Oddly enough, I can't recall how John's wife was dressed at that introduction; but if it had been anything outrageous I'm sure I'd have noticed.

Of their background I know nothing. Both spoke excellent English: John had hardly a trace of accent, but when his wife joined in the conversation I thought I heard a trace of some Northern, possibly Lancashire intonation. That really didn't seem at all possible. The odds are heavily against the KGB allowing one of their agents abroad to marry a native of the country in which he's stationed. She could have been an English expatriate he met and married in Russia; this again doesn't really ring true, although they both spoke Russian fluently. It remains a mystery so far as I'm concerned. Neither the Russians nor any of their satellites as a general rule permit both husband and wife to work abroad: one is left behind as a hostage against the other defecting. The only exception appears to be with Embassy staff, and John was definitely not in that category. Husband-and-wife teams such as the Rosenbergs and Krogers were recruited abroad.

As Lord Parker said to the jury in his summing-up at our trial:

> This has been a case which by its very nature has been full of intrigue. You may say it has all the characteristics of what is called a thriller. There is a great temptation for all of us to speculate about a number of ends which are left untied, and to turn ourselves into amateur detectives and wonder about this and that.

I was in the thick of the conspiracy, and although I can hardly be expected to agree with many of the Lord Chief Justice's remarks, I too, when I think of John and his wife, can only speculate about those ends which were left untied and remain so to this day.

Over coffee I casually mentioned that I'd booked for a winter sports holiday in Austria and wouldn't be in England until mid-January, so the January meeting had better not be arranged until I got back. After a meaning glance at John, Nikki asked if I was going anywhere near Salzburg. I said that Salzburg was quite some distance from Mayrhofen in the Tyrol, where I intended staying.

'How much is this holiday going to cost?'

I told them what the inclusive plane, coach and hotel fee would be, but didn't have a clue as to the spending money I'd require. Out of the blue Nikki said that he'd arrange for the cost of the trip to be paid, plus £100 spending money. Things had been going well, and he had noticed that I hadn't mentioned anything about a summer holiday. I ought to have a break. There wasn't much point in my telling him that I'd foregone my summer holiday that year simply in order to have a winter holiday: I was content to let someone finance the whole trip for me. On this cheerful note the party broke up and, as it was late, I returned to my hotel and went to bed.

Roman met me in December after coming back from a successful trip in the Russian cruiser *Ordzhonikidze*, and during this meeting made good Nikki's promise about financing my holiday in the Tyrol.

He threw off a few remarks about not being absolutely certain, but it was within the bounds of possibility that one of his superiors would also be having a holiday there and might even be staying at the same hotel. If that was so, would I mind talking to him? I couldn't see any objection to talking to the man, but on no account would I consent to take anything to him or bring anything back into this country. I was very firm about this. I was already sticking my neck out and risking prison in England, and I hadn't the slightest intention of breaking the law abroad or of facing an intensive search at the airport when I got home. Roman appeared to be hurt that I should dream of any such thing, and assured me that if by chance his superior did meet me it would only be for talks: it was by no means definite that he'd be there, anyhow.

So later that month I found myself at the Alte Poste Hotel in Mayrhofen enjoying my holiday, and by a chain of circumstances drifted into the company of three friendly Viennese, two women and a man, who were also staying there.

On about the fourth day after my arrival, while I was sitting alone in the café on the ski slopes, a man whom I'd only casually noticed in the hotel came across and engaged me in conversation over a lager. There were no elaborate passwords: he merely introduced himself as a friend of my London friends Nikki and John, said that he'd like to have talks with me, and could he come to my room in the evenings after it was thought I'd gone to bed?

This didn't suit me at all. I was making great headway with the odd girl out of the Viennese trio. She was sharing a room with her girl friend, and while the friend visited the man in his room, she had come only the previous night to my room for a goodnight drink. I didn't propose to let any Russian interfere with this beautiful friendship. I didn't tell him exactly why he couldn't come to my room, but remained adamant in the face of all his arguments until he gave in and consented to our meeting in his own room.

He had introduced himself as Gregory. He was very popular with the English holidaymakers in the hotel, and indeed spoke English very well, but with an accent which could have been cut with a knife. Unlike Roman and John, he would never have been able to pass himself off as English.

I strove to get Gregory to fix our talks as early as possible in the evenings by complaining that the mountain air made me sleepy, and succeeded. I saw to it that cakes, beer and slivovitz were left in my room, made sure the door was unlocked, and told my Viennese to help herself if I wasn't there when she arrived.

Gregory was reluctant to say anything about himself or where he had come from. I don't suppose I'd have believed him if he had told me. The only admission that did slip out indicated that he was a member of the GRU or KGB. Most of what he wanted to know was a repeat of things which Roman, Nikki and John had already asked me. There could have been one of two reasons: either he was checking on what I'd told the others, or was ascertaining that they had reported back correctly.

One evening there was a complete change of subject.

'Tell me all you know about the British Army's tank ranges and the regiment stationed at Bovington.'

This was a tall order. Bovington wasn't so far from my home in Dorset and I had seen tanks exercising there, but I scarcely knew the difference between a Chieftain tank and a Bren carrier. I was an ex-Naval man with little interest in such matters, and I could offer no help at all. At least, that was what *I* thought. Gregory thought differently. He produced an ordinary English road map of that part of Dorset and asked me to pinpoint vantage spots from which the tanks could be seen exercising and firing. I had to admit I didn't know for certain, but indicated a few places from which I thought there was a clear view, especially in the vicinity of Lawrence of Arabia's old cottage at Clouds Hill on the perimeter of the ranges, and places in the Purbeck Hills where I thought they might be observed through field-glasses. I also showed him on the map a few locations where I had happened to notice, from the roadway, tanks in their parking lots.

'Do you know any civilian fitters or electricians, or technicians who work in the maintenance workshops?'

He wasn't at all pleased when I told him I didn't.

His final instructions before leaving Mayrhofen were for me to find out all I could about the tank training grounds in Dorset—a commission I promptly forgot as soon as he had gone, until I was reminded about it in England at a later date.

Nothing he asked could not have been asked in England. Why had he come to a remote holiday resort to question me? He certainly had a holiday into the bargain, and perhaps was mixing business with pleasure. I did notice that he had formed an attachment to a middle-aged English divorcee at the hotel, and she appeared rather upset when he slipped away without telling her he was leaving. She would probably have been horrified if she had ever learned that her gentleman friend was a Russian Secret Service man.

Of all the agents I met, Gregory was the one I liked least. He had fixed ideas, and nothing could shake him. I never saw him again, and wasn't sorry.

I recall how angry he was—nowhere near as cool and tolerant as Bulganin and Khrushchev had shown themselves at the time—about Commander Crabb's exploit under the *Ordzhonikidze* when it visited Britain that previous Spring. If Crabb had succeeded in planting that limpet mine of his on the keel, it could have blown the ship sky-high, couldn't it? Knowing the whole story by then, I pointed out that it was accepted even by his own people that the mine was a small one and in any case wouldn't have exploded if the ship wasn't fitted with a certain type of ASDIC—which was what the British Admiralty were interested in, and what the whole thing was about.

But he would have none of it. 'Suppose it had exploded under a magazine—what then?'

He asked that same question over and over again.

People in this country also were still asking questions about Commander Lionel Phillip Kenneth Crabb, GM, OBE, RNVR, and they go on asking. Scarcely a year has gone by in which he has not been resurrected, in spite of the certainty expressed by the Chichester coroner in 1957 that the headless body on which he was holding an inquest was that of Lionel Crabb. The only problem was that the Coroner was unable to determine how he came to meet his death.

For the first time in any publication in the West I can tell the true story of how he was found on the bottom of the Soviet cruiser, and how he met his death.

Eccentric as he may have been, the man was a brilliant and fearless diver, and his heroic underwater exploits during the last war earned him a George Medal from King George VI. Books claiming that he is alive and well in Russia, and newspaper articles promoting him to Captain in the Soviet Navy, training underwater teams at the Black Sea naval dockyard of Sebastopol, are a grave discourtesy to this war hero's name.

I often wonder how different the turn of events might have been if Roman and I had not decided to 'get away from it all' one evening in the early Spring of 1956 and go off into the country for a drink at the Crown Inn at Puncknowle, in Dorset. There, I thought, we could relax and drink together without my having to explain away or introduce my friend to all and sundry.

It was in this remote country pub that Russian Intelligence got a line gratuitously on British Intelligence, neither seeking it nor expecting it. It just came out of the blue, an innocent yet so portentous remark from the lady friend of a naval diver who had also gone there to avoid friends and have a quiet drink where they wouldn't be known.

Chapter Five

The Truth About Crabb

Roman and I had settled down in the smallish bar, rather crowded with locals. Roman was listening, fascinated, to the strong Dorset dialect of the villagers, when a woman arrived who worked at the Underwater Detection Establishment. We knew each other quite well, and I also knew that the man with her was her current fancy, a Naval bod from the local shallow water diving team.

They hadn't expected to bump into anyone they knew, but decided to put a good face on it and asked if they could sit at our table, there being no room elsewhere. I introduced Roman as a friend of mine in the Merchant Navy whose ship was in Southampton and who had come to pay me a visit.

After a drink or two the boy friend excused himself and left the table to visit the lavatory, and when he'd departed I commented that he seemed very quiet tonight, quite different from what I'd imagined him: I hadn't known him to speak to before this meeting, but had seen and heard him from time to time in another pub I frequented.

The girl said, in effect, that we were to take no notice of his mood. He was a bit fed up, as he—or maybe it was *they*, I'm not sure after all this time—had been training for something special which had then been called off. He was still feeling a bit sore about it. The statement meant nothing to me, but Roman said idly:

'I wonder what it was?'

She didn't know—'But something silly, I suppose.'

Very soon after this Roman said it was about time he started on his way back to Southampton, which surprised me: we had intended staying in the pub until closing time.

Getting into the car, I suggested that as it was early we should call in at a pub in Abbotsbury which would amuse him, and have a snack as well: it was on our route home. But he said he wanted to go straight back to my place and collect his toilet gear, as he was returning to London immediately. When I queried this sudden change in our previous arrangements, he asked if I hadn't heard what the 'lady friend' had said. I replied that no-one had said anything of any great interest, and frankly I'd been rather bored by the two of them.

'The trouble with you,' he snapped, 'is that you don't take enough notice of what *is* said. We'd get on far better if you'd only keep your ears open.'

Thoroughly amazed by this outburst, I asked what on earth he was driving at. My own anger was rising at his tone.

'That diver chap who'd been training for something special,' he said, 'may be more important than you think.'

At a loss to understand what he could possibly have made of that fragment of conversation, I let the matter drop.

He collected his bits and pieces, and I drove him to Dorchester where he had left his car: they never drove right up to either the cottage or the caravan. I had one last go, quizzing him about this sudden departure.

He said: 'You do know who is coming to Portsmouth soon?'

Then I vaguely remembered having read that Marshal Bulganin and Nikita Khrushchev were to pay a state visit to this country in the near future. When I asked what this had to do with his abrupt return to London, he merely said that they would travel to Portsmouth in a Russian warship and there might be some connection. Perhaps the 'something special' referred to by the girl had in fact had nothing whatever to do with the Russian warship but, whether it had or not, it triggered off Roman's suspicions. He saw a possible relevance which was endorsed by the KGB and passed on to the Soviet Admiralty, who ordered additional Security precautions to be taken on the bottoms of the *Ordzhonikidze* and its attendant destroyers *Smotryashci* and *Sovershenny* whilst in British waters.

After the usual exchange of gun salutes at Spithead, the Soviet cruiser and destroyers with the Soviet Prime Minister, Bulganin, and Communist Party Secretary, Khrushchev, on board berthed at Kings Stairs, Portsmouth, on 18th April 1956. After the customary welcome by the Lord Lieutenant, the Lord Mayor, the Commander-in-Chief and other dignitaries, the two distinguished guests of this country left by special train for London, where they stayed at Claridges and did not return to the ships.

The whole world was intrigued by subsequent events. The Press gave the story saturation treatment. Everyone seemed to be in the picture and everyone had a watertight theory, with the exception of the Prime Minister, Sir Anthony Eden. How the Press got to know about it before the Prime Minister is anyone's guess: I've always maintained that they have a far better Intelligence service than the authorities have ever had.

Briefly, Crabb was missing after a dive to the bottom of the *Ordzhonikidze*. His accomplice, 'Bernard Smith', had vanished from the Sallyport Hotel in Old Portsmouth where he and Crabb had stayed, Inspector Lamport of the Portsmouth City Police having removed all traces of their names by extracting a page from the hotel register. Crabb's next appearance was without head or hands, the body still clad in his rubber diving suit, discovered by fishermen in Chichester Creek more than a year later—9th June 1957, to be precise.

On the day of the disappearance, Messrs B and K (as they were christened by the Press) paid the routine visit to the Cenotaph expected of all foreign dignitaries, went to see the Queen at Buckingham Palace, visited Number 10, lunched the Prime Minister and his cohorts at the Soviet Embassy, and returned to Downing Street for a conference. That evening, during a formal dinner, Khrushchev indulged in some mild mudslinging which showed he knew something Sir Anthony Eden didn't. It was not until the next morning that the British Prime Minister was put fully in the picture.

If the Secret Service pull off a job without being discovered, everything in the garden's lovely. But if a covert project comes unstuck and the foreign power against whom it's aimed finds out, then the Establishment deny all knowledge of it, wash their hands of those whose failure has been revealed...and later discipline the failures severely.

The Crabb fiasco was a routine job that went wrong, due perhaps to that young woman in a Dorset pub talking about something which meant more than she realised. Heads had to fall. A terrible outcry of indignation was raised in Parliament. Yet only a few months previously, when the Soviet cruiser *Sverdlov* visited Spithead in October 1955, Crabb is reliably reported to have been engaged by the Secret Service to do the self-same thing. This had been a success, so no outcry was raised. The second time the Service failed, as I was to do myself in due course, to observe the eleventh Commandment: 'Thou shalt not be found out.'

Although the Prime Minister was ignorant of what was going on, plenty of others must have known, including the maties of 'Pompey' Dockyard. Even in those days of somewhat slap-happy Security, someone must have issued Crabb and his accomplice 'Smith' with passes to enter the Dockyard; Crabb's diving gear had to go in and there had to be a place for him to don it unobserved (this was reported to be in a floating galley moored alongside the jetty); 'Smith' had to be allowed to hang around unchallenged by the Dockyard Police while he waited for Crabb to return from his dive; transport would have been organised to take their equipment away, curious onlookers had to be moved on, and so on. It could not have been concealed from a fair number of Portsmouth folk that something was afoot.

Khrushchev had an unpredictable temper, but apart from his cracks at that dinner and some snide remarks to 'certain underwater rocks' at a Press Conference in Central Hall, Westminster on 27th April just prior to his departure, he showed remarkable tolerance. For reasons known only to themselves the Russians reacted with admirable coolness to this act of discourtesy on their visiting warships. All that resulted was a formal note from the Soviet Embassy dated 4th May 1956, couched in the following moderate terms:

> During the stay of Soviet warships in Portsmouth, at 7.30 am on April 19th seamen on board the Soviet ships observed a frogman floating between the Soviet destroyers. The frogman, who wore black diving suit with flippers on his feet, was seen on the surface of the water for one to two minutes, and then dived alongside the destroyer *Smotryashci*.

The note went on to say that Captain Koltov, in command of the *Ordzhonikidze*, had raised the matter with the Commander-in-Chief, Portsmouth; and it asked for an explanation.

A speedy reply was forthcoming. On 9th May the British Government apologised for the incident:

> As has already been publicly reported, Commander Crabb carried out frogman tests, and, as is assumed, lost his life during these tests. The frogman, who, as reported in the Soviet Note, was discovered swimming between the Soviet destroyers, was to all appearances Commander Crabb. His presence in the vicinity of the destroyers occurred without any permission whatever, and Her Majesty's Government express their regret for this incident.

This expression of regret was charitably accepted by the Russians, and then the matter was closed.

The Press is reported to have squeezed a statement out of the Admiralty on 29th April in which it was said, among other things:

> Commander Crabb is presumed to be dead as the result of trials with certain underwater apparatus. The location of the trials was in Stokes Bay and it is nine days since the accident.

This was a clear admission that the Admiralty was in the picture at some stage. Had they been asked to undertake Crabb's mission in the first place, started training Naval divers to accomplish it, and then had second thoughts about the wisdom of the whole business? This could well have tied in with the lady friend's remark in the pub. It's extremely unlikely that the divers themselves would have known in advance the object of their training. Although the Admiralty would be glad to have certain information about Russian war vessels, there may well have been last-minute doubts about the desirability of putting Naval divers on the bottoms of such vessels, especially when an experienced ex-wartime officer of the RNVR was available to do the dirty work.

As events turned out, no-one in high places wanted to know anything about Crabb when the plot was discovered: he was disowned by everybody.

Although B and K were content to let the matter drop, the Opposition in the House of Commons were not so obliging. Their leader, Hugh Gaitskell, made the most of the political capital which had fallen into his lap when, in answer to a question from John Dugdale on 10th May, the Prime Minister declared:

> It would not be in the public interest to disclose the circumstances in which Commander Crabb is presumed to have met his death. While it is the practice for Ministers to accept responsibility, I think it is necessary in the special circumstances to make it clear that what was done was done without the authority or knowledge of Her Majesty's Ministers. Appropriate disciplinary steps are being taken.

The Secret Service being the Prime Minister's personal responsibility, this was a crafty bit of side-stepping. His failure to keep abreast of what the Department was doing provided Gaitskell with a sturdy weapon: he expressed, of course, the Opposition's displeasure at the way this host country had treated its visitors, but his attack was mainly a recrimination against the Prime Minister for not keeping more control over his Department.

But what *did* happen to Crabb?

As late as June 1969 a national Sunday newspaper was still claiming that Crabb was about to reappear. The suggestion 'from sources close to the Russian Foreign Ministry' was that Kapitan Crabb of the Russian Navy would soon be available for interview. No such interview ever materialised, and the story fizzled out. It may be revived again from time to time, but the results will be the same.

Crabb can never turn up because he dropped dead on board the cruiser *Ordzhonikidze* after his capture on 19th April 1956.

I was aware as early as July 1956 of the full story from the Soviet side. I could hardly have disclosed it at the time I was working for the Russians; then came a long period of imprisonment followed by a spell of parole. It is only now that I'm clear of Soviet Intelligence, prison and parole, that I'm at liberty to make these disclosures.

Within days of Roman's sudden departure from the pub en route for London, I received an urgent summons to a meeting at the lay-by on the Puddletown-Salisbury road, in the shape of advertising matter purporting to come from the Sun Life Assurance Company of Canada.

Roman met me there and earnestly told me that I was to find out all I could about the project from which the diver we'd met had been withdrawn. 'It's essential to get anything you can on it,' he said. 'It may be very important indeed.' It was useless to explain that I knew nothing about the shallow water diving team other than that such an organisation existed. I didn't even know where they were accommodated, or what craft they dived from. I didn't even know for sure that they were based nearby: they could be based at Portsmouth and come to Portland only as necessary. It was difficult trying to get Roman to appreciate that the diving team was naval and my department was civilian, so that apart from working for the same firm—the Admiralty—we had nothing in common. However I promised to try, knowing full well there was little I could do. In fact, in the end I did nothing at all about it.

Although he had mentioned the visit of B and K a few days

previously, I couldn't really follow Roman's train of thought. It wasn't until the Crabb episode hit the headlines that I began to get a glimmering.

It was late July before I met Roman again. In the meantime I had seen Nikki a couple of times, and in reply to my questions about Roman he merely said that he was on leave and appeared not to want to discuss the matter any further.

When I did meet Roman it was near Blackbush airport, in the car park of the Ely Hotel. At that time Blackbush was a small operational airfield with the control on one side of a narrowish road and the hangars and workshops on the other, with access to wooded countryside. After tea at the hotel he suggested a stroll, and it was then that I heard the truth for the first time. We had gone into the scrubland where we could be neither seen nor overheard. After this lapse of time I can't hope to give Roman's account verbatim, but the details themselves are still clear enough in my mind.

He started off by giving me a lecture on the necessity of taking note of everything I heard. The most casual remark could lead to something of the utmost importance. All this led up to him giving himself a pat on the back for his astuteness in following up and reporting the innocent remark we had heard in the Crown at Puncknowle.

What he didn't say in so many words, but conveyed to me with dark hints, was that I was by now up to my neck in the espionage game, compromised up to the hilt, and so in no position to repeat to anyone what he was about to tell me.

He claimed that as a direct result of his visit to Dorset the *Ordzhonikidze* had been fitted out with two wire jackstays running the full length of the ship below the waterline as a support for underwater sentries to hold on to against the strong tides they would encounter in Portsmouth Harbour. Six men would guard the ship's bottom at all times and all states of the tide.

They didn't have long to wait. B and K arrived on 18th April, and the very next morning these precautions bore results.

In spite of their alertness, when Crabb appeared for the first time they lost him in the murky waters of the Dockyard. Some minutes later he was encountered again, and during the ensuing struggle his oxygen was turned off for long enough to make him pass out. His unconscious body was then hastily hauled on board and carried below out of sight. By this time he was recovering consciousness, but on being taken to the sick bay he passed out again. After medical treatment he recovered and, in answer to questions, began to make a confession. During this questioning he collapsed and died.

I asked whether force had been used on him. Roman assured me it hadn't. His opinions tied in with some of the stories which spread in this country later, about Crabb being in poor physical condition and on the verge of alcoholism. Recovering consciousness in strange surroundings, he was in no fit state to face up to any stringent interrogation. To have used force on him would have defeated the questioners' objectives. They were afraid of him dying—and he beat them to it by doing just that.

'How do you know all this?' I asked Roman.

The answer was straight: 'Because I was there.'

This was verified later by a man I met a couple of times in Dublin and also, later still, by Gordon Lonsdale. From each of these three sources the story did not vary.

The intention of getting him on board was twofold: to find out what the British wanted to know about the ship, and to be in the position of humiliating them by making a signal that someone had been caught on the ship's bottom and would they please come and collect him. This would have been a masterly stroke. Unfortunately that bit went all wrong: with Crabb dying on their hands, the Russians could now find themselves being accused of his death, which hadn't been the plan at all.

It was a delicate situation. What were they to do with the body?

It was decided to put him back in the water, lightly secured to the hull by the Russian equivalent of spun yarn, so that by the time the ship had got under way and proceeded a mile or so the yarn would chafe and the body would come adrift. As things turned out, the body remained in the sea for fourteen months, probably entangled in a submarine cable or a wreck.

Having heard this much, I was anxious to know what the object of Crabb's mission had been.

As a naval diver myself during part of my RN career, I had trained at Portsmouth Dockyard and knew as well as anyone the lack of visibility on a ship's keel. Add to this the fact that the *Ordzhonikidze* was shielded from the light by the Kings Stairs jetty, and also that her attendant destroyers were tied up to her other side, and it's plain that Crabb's vision would have been seriously impaired: and if it's true that she drew more than 18-ft of water then he would have been completely in the dark while underneath the bottom. If he had been allowed to carry a light, which is questionable, it would have been of a pretty ineffective type. In such conditions he would have been relying almost entirely on his sense of touch. With six sentries forming a reception committee, that did him about as much good as a telltale light would have done.

Roman had already declared that he was actually on board the *Ordzhonikidze* at the time of Crabb's capture. When he went on to display an intimate knowledge of ASDICs and a firm grasp on naval matters in general, I grew more and more convinced that he must at some stage have been a Russian naval officer, probably seconded to the GRU and later the KGB. He was steeped in naval matters: they had undoubtedly chosen the right man for this job.

It appears that during the interrogation Crabb had disclosed that he had entered the Harbour with a small limpet mine secured to him. In accordance with his training he had automatically slipped it from his body and let it sink to the seabed when he was pounced on.

'But they weren't going to blow up the cruiser at Kings Stairs?' I burst out.

No. There had been no intention of blowing it up. British Intelligence wanted to know if the Russians had caught up with our sophisticated ASDIC programme, and particularly whether the cruiser was fitted with the equivalent of Type—. I should explain briefly that ASDIC (now called SONAR) is a submarine detection device, projecting through the ship's bottom encased in a retractable dome. To find its target it transmits an impulse through the water which is reflected by anything that gets in the way and returns a message to the transmitting vessel. (This is an over-simplification, but I'm not going to risk discussing all the modern extensions and refinements.) If the *Ordzhonikidze* carried the type of ASDIC the British wanted to know about, it would emit a certain impulse peculiar to that kind of set. The limpet mine had been fitted with a device which, picking up this impulse, would explode the mine. Although this would cause no injury to anyone on board, it would temporarily slow the ship down, and this would be observed by aircraft on the lookout for just that thing. If, however, the limpet mine did not explode after a certain number of hours—I think Roman gave it three days, though that seems rather a long period—this would indicate that the Russians didn't have the type of ASDIC concerned, and the mine would detach itself and fall harmlesly into the depths.

In normal circumstances it is quite certain that a man of Crabb's calibre would have given no information about himself or his mission to the Russians. But in his low state of health and, by all accounts, dangerously affected by alcohol, he was unable to stand up to the traumatic experience of being overpowered under the sea, restored to consciousness on a foreign cruiser amidst unfriendly faces, and subjected to stern questioning, scrupulously correct as it may have been. No wonder he confessed.

And no wonder Roman was so pleased with himself.

Chapter Six

Meetings and Landings

One Saturday evening John began to ask me questions about the state of the bottom of the cliffs at low water, near where my caravan was situated on Portland. I said I didn't think there was anything visible, as the cliffs rose sheer from the sea and I was pretty sure there were only rocks at the bottom. But within a few hundred yards was Church Ope Cove, where the pebbly shore was exposed at most states of the tide, if not all.

'Could a boat land there?'

'I've seen boats land,' I recollected. 'Providing the sea's calm and you've got the right wind, there shouldn't be any difficulties.'

John was constantly referring to notes he had brought with him, and painstakingly writing down my answers to his questions.

I explained that to get down to Church Ope Cove there were man-made steps from the cliff-top to the sea. The number of people about would depend on the time of year and weather. There were a number of beach huts in the vicinity, but from late Autumn until early Spring there would rarely be anyone about after dark.

John asked if I could meet him again the following Saturday. I demurred. Bunty, whom I was meeting regularly and who still knew absolutely nothing about these activities of mine, would be curious if I made excuses for not seeing her on two consecutive Saturdays: I was getting hard pressed to contrive plausible excuses as it was. So it was agreed that we'd meet at the usual lay-by on the Salisbury road a week the following Monday.

When I met John that Monday evening I was astounded at the proposal he made. Quite simply it was that I should place two red leading lights on the cliff to guide a boat in. I was to meet two passengers from the boat and identify myself by asking:

'Did you get any fish?'

'None at all.'

'What a pity.'

Then I would convey them in my car to Blandford Forum car park. There I must look out for another car with a white paper square on the windscreen, park as close to it as possible...and do nothing else.

When the occupants of the other car were satisfied we were not being observed, they would transfer the passengers from my car to theirs. I was then to drive off immediately. On no account was I to question my passengers, and would speak to them only to give essential instructions. The only foreseeable danger to me would be at the actual landing and the walk up the steps of the cliff. If questioned after they were safely landed I was to say that I'd been out for a walk, and the other two, who could speak English, would also say that they'd been walking and that we were strangers to each other.

I didn't like the idea, and told John so. But after a while I agreed.

There were to be three alternative nights for the landing when no naval exercises were taking place. The moon had to be right, and much would depend on the weather. John supplied me with the landing lights, electric and well screened so as not to throw a light landward. My instructions were that on my return I was to recover them and throw them into the sea over the edge of the cliffs, by which time the batteries would have been long exhausted. If I sensed danger, the lights were not to be placed; if there was only a temporary setback, I was to go to a point above the cliff near my caravan and make a series of dot-dot-dash-dash with my torch on a given compass bearing, when the attempt would be made the following evening. There was a whole series of signals for various eventualities, which I have since forgotten.

Several reasons were given for the choice of Church Ope Cove. Landing there would not entail the boat having to enter Portland breakwater; the cove was not visible from the Coastguard lookout post or Portland Bill lighthouse; living nearby, I wouldn't attract undue attention if I was seen in the vicinity; there was secluded parking at the top of the steps; and the leading lights could be placed unobserved. Also, as a last resort in dire emergency, the passengers could hide out in my caravan, though it was essential to get them off the island as soon as possible.

In the event of the operation being frustrated on the seaward side, there'd be no safe way of letting me know: it would be foolhardy to flash a light in my direction. If there was any delay, I was to wait for forty minutes and then extinguish and remove the leading lights, but in these circumstances I wasn't to destroy them by tossing them over the cliff. Provided I got no message to the contrary, the attempt was to be made at the same time the next night.

Having reluctantly agreed to take part in this escapade my obvious question was: when and at what time was it likely to take place, and how would I be notified?

This had all been worked out. I would receive yet another sample of advertising matter through the post. On receipt of this I was to make a point of going every evening thereafter to the country inn I used near Weymouth, making sure of being on the premises at 8.45-pm. A telephone call would come through as close as possible to that time and the caller would ask if Harry was there that evening. The landlord, landlady and the odd-job man, a Mr Croad, all knew me as Harry. The message was that a cousin in the area on business that week wanted to get in touch with me. It was necessary to have some story of this kind, as in those country pubs it was more than likely that the caller would be asked: 'Who's speaking, please?'

On answering the phone, after a bit of idle chatter I'd ask, for the benefit of anyone who happened to be listening: 'Where can I see you?'

'Be at Dorchester station at...' would be the reply.

The time which he then gave would be the precise time I was to switch on the landing lights.

I made it clear to John that, although I frequently went to this pub, I didn't want to be tied down to being there at a quarter to nine night after night over a long period. He assured me that once I got the advertising matter the landing would be imminent.

Nothing happened for nearly a week, and I was beginning to think they had decided the plan for this enterprise was a bit too ambitious. Then on the seventh day the advertising leaflets arrived. The thought of it preyed on my mind all day. When the office closed I hurried to the caravan to have a quick meal, change and get away before any friends chose to drop in for a drink and listen to records, as they sometimes did in this isolated community. This was a night when I could do without companions.

The weather was miserable. I drove round the country lanes, filling in time and wondering apprehensively what the night might have in store for me. At last I headed for the pub, and was settling down to drink with some cronies when I was summoned to the phone. This is it, I thought.

The message I received stunned me. I was told to be at Dorchester station at 11-pm that very same evening.

It had never occurred to me that the operation would have been scheduled to take place with only a couple of hours' notice to me. Feeling all keyed up, I tried to sound delighted over the phone, downed my drink, and dashed back to Portland, topping up the car with petrol on the way. I muffled myself up in my duffle coat and trudged down the steps to Church Ope Cove to make sure that the coast was clear and that there were no courting couples on the seats or anglers fishing from the shore. Then I parked the car ready for a quick getaway and explored the cliff-top, from which I could see that the Shambles lightship beam was bright: despite the dirty night, visibility would be good.

I retraced my steps and at exactly 11-pm switched on the leading lights.

Then there was a long, agonizing wait. I smoked cigarette after cigarette and watched the lights getting dimmer and dimmer as the batteries ran down. Full of apprehension as to why the boat hadn't shown up, I carried out my instructions and extinguished what light remained. Back in the caravan I replaced the batteries and went to bed, wondering what had gone wrong. The only bright spot was that there hadn't been a soul about near the cove.

Next day at the office seemed endless. Constantly in my mind was the thought that the whole performance would have to be repeated this coming evening.

Once again I hurried home, had a hasty meal, and checked that the lights would work again. I thought it as well to go to the pub in case any other cryptic message came for me, also to avoid any chance visitors. There was no message. I left the pub early and returned to Portland, and went through the same routine in case the landing was about to be made this evening.

I didn't have long to wait before there was a muffled noise which I thought must be a motor-boat engine. I left my hiding place and got down to the water's edge just in time to pick out in the darkness a boat, with two figures scrambling out. They had had excellent training: without effort they smoothly turned the craft nose to sea, gave it a push, and it was away, leaving them to their fate. The landing was accomplished, it seemed, in a matter of seconds.

I made my presence known by asking if they'd got any fish; and so made the acquaintance of two more Russian spies.

They both wore Wellingtons and had their shoes secured round their necks. I led the way up the steps without further word, and was greatly relieved when we got to the top and to my car unobserved, although the likelihood of interruption had been remote. One of them asked where it would be convenient to get out of their boots and put their shoes on. I assured them we were safe now, and they could do it right away. They put the Wellingtons in the boot of my Renault, and we set off.

I drove up through Wakeham to Easton, thence to Priory Corner, down to Fortuneswell and Chiswell, and so on to the causeway, the only road off Portland.

And there we were confronted by a police road block.

This hadn't been there when I returned to Portland from the pub a few hours ago. I knew what it meant, but my passengers didn't, and I could sense their tension. In the event of a prisoner escaping from the Verne prison or a youth making a dash for it from Portland Borstal, this road block was manned immediately by police and by warders from whichever of the two establishments was concerned. All cars leaving Portland would be searched for the escaper. We had nothing to fear, as in such cases the warders know exactly who they're looking for, and the police are there only to force cars to stop, or to give chase in a police car in the event of someone ignoring their halt sign. But my passengers might, in a panic, do something silly.

It was very dark. When the POLICE HALT sign came up in my headlights only two hundred yards from the check point I had to do some quick explaining.

'Act natural. Say nothing. They are not looking for us—a prisoner has escaped, they know his face, you won't be questioned and you won't have to get out of the car.'

By this time we were at the road block. I wound my window down. Noboby but me appeared to be breathing.

A torch was flashed on us by a warder, with a policeman standing by.

'Thank you, sir. Goodnight.'

We were waved on. It was as simple as that. The men in uniform could hardly have been expected to guess that of the three occupants of the car two were Russian spies who had just landed from a submarine or a trawler under the not so watchful eyes of the Navy.

I don't know what would have happened if the police had in fact been waiting for us. In spite of my reassurance I had had, during those few fraught moments, the fear that my companions would somehow give us away, anyway. For myself, I'd been vastly relieved to see the warders and know the road block wasn't for us. I haven't always been so pleased to see them!

If the escape had taken place in the daytime I'd have been aware of it: a black flag used to be hoisted over the Council Offices and over Portland Police Station to warn local residents that a breakout had taken place. It was unfortunate that someone had chosen this night of all nights to make a run for it.

Going through Weymouth, I mentioned the possibility of our being stopped again, and emphasised that in the event of any questioning they should take their cue from me. In fact we were flagged down at Warmwell Crossroads by a motor-cycle policeman who peered into the car and waved us on immediately. Nothing else alarming happened on our journey to Blandford Forum. The only car in the park was the one I had been instructed to pick out. After a decent interval, John came over to enquire if we had encountered any trouble. I told him nothing had gone wrong. The passengers were transferred and I was about to drive away when I remembered the Wellington boots. They were taken out, and then I was free at last to hurry back to Portland.

Next morning I picked up Bunty at her home as usual and drove her to work. I couldn't help speculating what she and others in the Underwater Detection Establishment would have said if they could have known about the two immigrants who had set foot on our shores not so many hours ago.

When the operation was first mooted, I hadn't liked the idea at all. But in spite of my trepidation I did, in fact, begin to look forward to it. An exploit like this, and the meetings we had, and the challenge of obtaining material to photograph under tricky circumstances made such a change from humdrum office life on low pay.

I did my utmost to find out more about the two who landed on Portland, but ran into a wall of silence any time I mentioned them. It's possible that they passed out of the ken of John and Roman when they reached their destination, and even Roman didn't know what their task was. I'd be hard pressed to describe the newcomers, as I only saw them under street lighting, and in a car at that. But one thing stands out clearly in my memory. Each wore what appeared to be an English, well cut coat and suit, and they were glad of my English cigarettes to smoke on the journey: it was as though they had landed with nothing in their possession but the clothes they stood up in.

Neither could I find out what kind of a vessel they had launched from. I'm inclined to think it would have been a submarine, but I've yet to hear of a submarine which carries a motor-boat, even an inflatable one. When I asked John about it and tried to get him to say whether it was a sub or a trawler, his only answer was another question: 'Which do you think would get through a radar screen more easily?' Meaning, I suppose, that it was a submarine.

Much later, I was told that the first message I received to meet the passengers, when nobody turned up, was a dummy run to test the leading lights and, I suppose, my reliability: they wanted to check the timing and above all to know from the seaward side that the plans made would be carried out to the letter.

'Is there anything to prevent you going over to Ireland?' The question came out of the blue from Roman some six or eight weeks after the two men had come ashore at Church Ope Cove.

One thing was certain about this little lot: at no meeting could I ever be sure what they'd want me to do next, or where they'd want me to go. During the summer it had been suggested that I should go to Gibraltar. This arose from a chance remark to the effect that Naval Dockyards abroad, such as those at Gibraltar, Malta, Singapore and Hong Kong, had a complement of technical staff and key workmen sent out on a tour of duty from Home Dockyards. Soviet Intelligence must have mulled this over, for soon afterwards I was asked to spend a holiday in Gibraltar. While there I could look up any friends I had from home bases, and lead the conversation round to whether there was anything in the rumour that the Dockyard had laid a cable across the Straits of Gibraltar with a listening device on the inshore end to pick up engine and propellor noises from vessels passing through. Evidently the Russians weren't keen for it to be known when their submarines and other warships entered or left the Mediterranean at the Atlantic end.

I wasn't at all enthusiastic about this suggestion. Having been to Gibraltar many times in my Navy career, I would have put it very low on my list of places in which to spend a happy holiday. Apart from the various service establishments there was nothing there— nothing but a few apes, cheap booze and smokes, and a very crowded beach. I turned down the idea, and when they got argumentative I pointed out that people I was likely to meet there would think I needed my head examined if I went from one Naval base to another for a holiday. I couldn't and wouldn't be persuaded; and I didn't go.

Thinking that the remark about a trip to Ireland must mean something on the same lines as the Gibraltar suggestion, I was somewhat cagey in my reply. I knew a submarine training flotilla operated from Northern Ireland, but I'd be unable to tell them anything about it as I had absolutely no contacts there. I liked Ireland, always have done, and wouldn't mind going there. But definitely not to seek information for them: anyone else would be just as capable of doing that as I would.

Anyway, were we talking about Northern Ireland or Eire?

To my surprise Roman said it was Dublin he had in mind. There was no question of my being compromised in any way.

Being a great consumer of the waters of the Liffey in its more palatable form, I pricked up my ears and was prepared to listen to more. At that stage he either didn't know exactly what was involved, or made out that he didn't, for all he would tell me was that if I agreed and we could fix a date, I'd be booked in at the Gresham Hotel under the name of Charles Casey of Bristol. My hotel bill would be taken care of, I was to have my meals brought up to my room, and at exactly 9-pm I would answer a knock on my bedroom door, when a certain gentleman would enquire if I'd had a pleasant journey.

'Yes,' I was to reply, 'but I could do with a drink.'

'Not a soft one, I hope,' would be his next line.

Then I was to ask for an Irish coffee, and invite him to enter. He would then ring for drinks to be brought, and until they arrived and the waiter departed we were only to exchange pleasantries. After that we'd discuss whatever it was he wanted to see me about.

Curiosity was probably the main factor in my decision to accept. It happened, very neatly, that Bunty had arranged to spend the following weekend away from home at a friend's place. I fancy she'd decided that if I could flit off mysteriously for the odd weekend now and then, she could do the same. I asked Roman if the trip could be arranged for that time, explained it would coincide with my fiancée's weekend with friends, and there would be much less fuss this way: there was another part of my life just as important to me as their demands, and I was straining things to the limit already on their behalf. Roman agreed. I arranged to take the following Friday off—I had accumulated a certain amount of leave and could afford this—to go to Bristol, take an Aer Lingus flight, return on the Sunday and motor back to Weymouth.

Roman settled the plane booking and said he would personally see me off from Bristol. No doubt he would also phone Dublin to say that I was airborne and on my way. Departure from Bristol rather than from London fitted in with the fictitious address and hotel booking in the name of Mr Charles Casey.

During the ensuing week I let it be known that I was thinking of going north at the weekend to visit relatives, and as I wanted to start after the office closed on the Thursday I'd require the day off on Friday. This was OK'd without hesitation.

Everything went as planned. As Mr Charles Casey I duly presented myself at the Gresham, had a quick bath, and changed. There was plenty of time before my appointment. Although I had been instructed to order my meals in my room, nothing had been said about having a drink. So down I went and got stuck into a glass of Irish whiskey.

During my second, I found myself in conversation with a striking looking brunette—probably on the wrong side of forty, but no matter: where beauty and charm are, age matters not. It was fairly vague, inconsequential chat until she asked if I knew what Irish coffee was. It might have been an innocent remark, and certainly wasn't an out-of-the-way one in that setting. But could she just possibly be the 'certain gentleman' who was to visit my room at 9-pm? I explained what Irish coffee was, and she said she'd try one after dinner.

She eventually departed and I went to my room, ordered a meal to be sent up, and after it had been cleared away waited for my visitor.

Precisely at 9-pm the expected knock came on my door. Half expecting to meet the attractive brunette, I hurried to open it...and found to my dismay a shortish, pudgy, balding man in his early fifties carrying a document case and what turned out to be a small portable radio receiver.

We shook hands while reciting our identification phrases, and he came into my room. He said he had ordered drinks to be sent up, mine being a Jameson's whiskey.

'How do you know I drink Jameson's?' I asked.

'Don't tell me you've already forgotten your companion before dinner.'

He refused to tell me who she was, and with the arrival of the waiter with the drinks we dropped the subject. It wasn't resumed.

On the departure of the waiter, my visitor locked the door and placed the portable radio against it, turned down fairly low. This, he explained, would make any eavesdropper's task difficult: not that he expected anyone to show any interest in us, but it was as well to be on the safe side. It was standard practice: even in the caravan or the Weymouth cottage my Soviet visitors always insisted on the radio or gramophone being on while we discussed things.

He began by saying he wasn't at liberty to tell me who he was, but for convenience I could call him Tony if I liked. He had broken his journey in Eire for the express purpose of meeting me and conveying the congratulations of his superiors for the success on the South Coast recently. Apparently it was inadvisable for him to go to London.

I knew there had to be more to it than that. They wouldn't get me over to Ireland and send a man from God knows where just to say 'Thank you'.

He gave no idea where he was from or where he was travelling to. At a guess I'd say that the talk about his breaking his journey wasn't true, but that he had come to Eire specially for this meeting.

Which brought me back to the question of what it was really all about.

From his document case he now produced an envelope containing tracings or photographic copies of Admiralty charts. These had been transposed on to paper so thin that they were all contained in one foolscap envelope. Charts are usually produced on heavy quality cartridge paper. My visitor was certainly travelling light.

He questioned me closely about the police road block on the Portland causeway. Was this a frequent occurrence? Why hadn't I suggested a disembarkation point where, in the event of a prison breakout, there would have been less risk of detection by the police? I tried to convince him that there wasn't the slightest possible danger to anyone passing the check point other than to the escaper: I'd been through many such, dozens of times, and the routine was always the same — a quick look in the car, sometimes in the boot, and nothing else. No questions were asked. The warders knew who they were looking for, and neither they nor the police had time to worry about anything else on such occasions.

He wasn't convinced. He insisted that we settled on another landing place.

This was the first intimation I'd had that there were to be more arrivals. I had to watch while he pointed out on his charts various likely spots. At least, *he* thought they were likely. All of them were unsuitable, some ridiculously so, being either right under the eyes of the Coastguards or entailing a long walk through rough country in the dark to the getaway transport. I insisted that nowhere else could leading lights be placed with the near certainty of remaining unobserved, and in any case I wasn't going to stick my neck out trying to set up such an operation anywhere other than Church Ope Cove on Portland. If they were determined to run risks elsewhere, they'd have to get somebody else for the job.

His reaction was to ask sharply if I thought 'they' were such bad navigators that they had to be guided ashore by lights. I pointed out that it had been their own idea in the first place, and they had been the ones to provide me with the lights and with spare batteries. He calmed down, and said that next time lights would not be used: there had been a change of policy.

In which case, I said, there'd be no need for my services.

I was wrong. It would be necessary, he said, for the 'guests' to be received by someone well acquainted with the area and able to supply transport. Who was better qualified than I?

Then followed a long discussion on the most suitable spot. He was keen on West Bay, but I vetoed this, as the Chesil Bank would make an extra boat trip necessary. Also it was under the eyes of the Coastguards, and access to transport wasn't easy. So it had to be east of Weymouth. We had almost settled for Osmington—it would probably be deserted, there was good parking close to the sea—until I remembered his worries about the police check point. If there should be a breakout on the night we worked at Osmington, we'd have to pass the check point at Warmwell Crossroads. So that was out. After interminable study of the terrain and considerable argument, and after my assurance that the Coastguard look-out posts didn't have radar, we settled for Lulworth Cove. All this, of course, without reference to those who would have to make the landing.

He didn't seem unduly concerned about the depth of water outside. It looked all right to me. The one drawback was that the time would have to be selected when the Army was not firing out to sea. We agreed that disembarkation should take place inside the cove itself but as close as possible to the entrance. For the sake of getting the arrivals away quickly, it should be on the boat's port side. This time I would be required to convey them to Ringwood in the New Forest instead of to Blandford Forum. The same password routine was to be used. No signals would be made this time unless there was a chance of danger from the landward: if anything went wrong at my end, I was to drive to the high ground on Durdle Dor, face the sea, and switch on the car headlights for five seconds every thirty seconds. To save confusion there would be no alteration in the alerting procedure save that the advertising matter this time would be from the World Record Club, and I was to check for a pinhole in the centre. The phone call from my 'cousin' to the pub would be the same.

This talk had taken us nearly to midnight. I thought we had finished for the night, when he brought out a print of a chart of Portland Dockyard and asked me to show him exactly where the Underwater Detection Establishment was situated. I was a bit surprised by this, as I knew quite well that Nikki had photographed it from the high ground overlooking the harbour, and furthermore I had long since furnished a full description of the layout of the Establishment complete with rough sketches identifying the workshops, drawing offices, stores, laboratories and other offices. There was a secondary block, South Block, of which I knew little: I seldom had occasion to go there, and consequently could furnish no information. When I came to study Tony's chart I found that the whole set-up was just off the rim of the picture, so the best I could do was point out roughly where it lay in relation to his chart.

'Is the building well guarded at night?'

He couldn't understand my mirth at this question. It shook him when I told him that the only person in the place after the staff had gone home was a solitary night watchman.

'But surely, with all those secrets, there must be armed sentries.'

I told him I worked there, and knew, and that he had to take my word for it. His disbelief was understandable: in Russia, Poland, and most other foreign countries almost every Government building has its armed police or militia on guard.

'Would it be possible to get inside one night to have a look round?'

Nothing, I replied, could be easier. But he must understand that the Establishment was actually inside the Dockyard, which was patrolled by a few Admiralty Police at night. Once entry to the Dockyard had been gained and these avoided, it would be a piece of cake. A door or window would have to be left open for a quiet entry, but that was a very minor detail.

I went on to explain that not much would be gained from getting into the Establishment. All papers and confidential material were locked away each evening in filing cabinets and safes, and unless one had expert knowledge there was no way of interpreting objects seen in the workshops and elsewhere. He replied that 'they' would be the best judge of that.

'Do the draughtsmen remove their drawings from the drawing boards before going home?' was the next question.

I couldn't reply with any accuracy. It would have been thought a bit odd if I'd been two storeys up in the drawing office at going-home time instead of being at the ready in true Civil Service fashion, waiting for the 5.15 rush.

Then came a long feasibility study on how to get into the Dockyard undetected. Entering it from the harbour would be easy, but would entail hiring a boat, which I didn't consider prudent. Entry from the landward side would be comparatively easy except that it meant clambering down a hill almost completely overgrown with brambles, which would take some time to shove through. It had at any rate been easy enough on one occasion for an escaper from Verne Prison, which overlooks the Dockyard, to stumble inadvertently into the Dockyard one night—and to be found asleep in the paint store the following morning. A little-used railway line with a high fence on the Dockyard side ran parallel to the landward side for maybe two-thirds of a mile, with a bridge crossing the road adjacent to UDE, which would be most useful providing a rope ladder could be placed for climbing back on to it. After several other methods of entry had been analysed, this was the one chosen as the likeliest route.

Then came the question I had been waiting for. If it was decided to go inside the Establishment one night, would I assist?

Before giving an answer there were several things I wanted to know. The chief one was what would happen to the night watchman in the unlikely event of his coming across anyone prowling around inside the place: I knew all the watchmen, for they worked day shifts as well, and on no account was I going to be a party to any one of them being clobbered.

Strict orders would be given, I was promised, that if the night watchman discovered anyone he should be overpowered and tied up with absolutely no violence.

I agreed, then, to assist, provided the venture was timed for around 10 pm, when the watchman would be having his supper break in the messengers' room.

So ended the meeting in Dublin.

During the years in which I had ample time to think over my

past misdeeds, I came to the conclusion that this man was almost certainly the Director of all Soviet spy operations in this country, and even perhaps in all Western Europe. My theory is that although he knew all those working under him, the others knew only *of* him and didn't meet him in England. All directions and communications between them would be conducted by means of 'dead letter boxes', or even microfilm, so that he was as safe as he could possibly be. I think he was paymaster for all the groups in the field, co-ordinator between these groups, and that he could well have been the one to whom the Code Book went which could not be found on our arrests.

To ensure his safety even further, he would not meet any of his top operatives in person in the United Kingdom: they would meet on the Continent or in Eire, in safer surroundings. There was really no need for him to have set a meeting-place with me in Dublin other than reluctance to get too close to the real scene of operations. From that distance he wanted completely to satisfy himself on the feasibility of carrying out what his superiors had in mind. Roman, John or, later, Lonsdale never delved quite so deeply into possible snags when we were discussing future projects. Probably 'Tony'—or whatever he was called, if he was ever called any one thing for very long—had been in the West for some years masquerading as a businessman. I never did discover who the charming brunette was, nor did I ever see her again. One thing is pretty certain, though: my meeting with her was no coincidence. It was possible that 'Tony' had seen me having a drink and, disconcerted, sent her hastily along to make sure that I had no opportunity of getting into conversation with anyone else.

Back to work on Monday with no one having had the slightest suspicion that I had been out of the country—not even Bunty.

Chapter Seven

Enter Gordon Lonsdale

About the time of my meeting Gregory in Austria, the Underwater Detection Establishment was having a seagoing tender, *Decibel*, fitted out as a floating laboratory at Bolsom's Yard, Hamworthy, Poole. To me this was of small account and I didn't even mention it to Nikki or Roman.

At one meeting I had been asked if expenditure on various projects and trials for the next financial year was likely to be increased. Naturally I couldn't give an answer off the cuff, but I said I'd find out. I didn't tell them how easy this was: it merely meant having a look at the sketch estimates in course of preparation for the forthcoming year.

I made a condensed version of these and handed over the results. On the list appeared the name *Decibel*. Roman asked what this vessel was and what it would do. All I could tell him was that she'd be a tender on which equipment of various kinds would be tested under seagoing conditions. Being neither a scientist nor a technician, I had no means of knowing the nature of the test equipment, though it was fairly common knowledge that the *Decibel* was being fitted out with laboratories. Then came the inevitable question: would there or would there not be an armed guard on board? They seemed to have this notion on the brain. The answer was, as usual, easy enough: there would be no armed guard. The vessel was in any case at that moment in a private commercial shipyard, and would remain there for another week or so until her completion.

Would it be possible for Roman to see her?

I assured him that nothing could be simpler. I told him the best vantage point in Poole for a really good look. A few days later I was summoned to meet him at the lay-by on the Puddletown-Salisbury road, and there he made arrangements to meet me in Poole the next Saturday so that I could show him from my car the shipyard where the *Decibel* lay. This I did. It was all quite straightforward.

Then I was asked to meet him again, after dark, in my car. This time he turned up with another man and told me to take them to the shipyard. They got out. I was to cruise around for exactly forty minutes and pick them up again at the same place. I carried out these instructions, and on my return didn't have long to wait after the appointed time: they soon reappeared, and I drove them to a car park, left them there, and went off to Weymouth.

Subsequently Roman told me that they had got on board the ship and taken a number of flashlight photographs of the interior. His companion was a London locksmith on whom they called for odd jobs—in this case to open up the laboratories and any other doors which might be required. I observed that the photographs would be pretty useless as there was no test equipment on board the ship in its present state. But, pleased as ever with himself, Roman assured me that these pictures would be evaluated by people whose business it was to piece together small details and thus come to conclusions about the overall picture. In this instance I think he took a needless risk: but he was a man not afraid to take risks for the minutest particle of information. Nothing was too small for him to add to his store.

To make it even more absurd, immediately after completion at Bolsom's in Poole the tender came round to Weymouth and was moored at the quay where members of the public could, and did, go to see her. Photographs and a fuller description than I had been able to supply of her future role as tender to the UDE appeared in the local evening paper.

It was not until some eighteen months after meeting Gregory that I thought any more about Bovington Camp and the tank ranges.

By this time I had left the caravan and was back in my cottage. Peggy had wasted no time after the divorce came through: she had been going around with another man for quite some time, and married him the very day the divorce was made absolute. I hadn't jibbed at her staying in the place while she was on her own, but with the best will in the world I couldn't see why the two of them should have a free home in my property, and asked her to leave so that I could return to it and be a bit more comfortable than I had been recently.

There was a pub not far away which became my local, and one evening I was called to the telephone there. The landlord told me my cousin was calling. I wondered which cousin it was this time! In fact it was John phoning from Dorchester—really at Dorchester this time—and asking if he could come to the pub and see me. We made it a rule for security reasons that no calls were to be made to my cottage just on the long chance that my phone might be tapped. The only exception was in a real emergency, when a 'wrong number' procedure would be operated: my number was Upwey 784, and if, when I answered, the caller enquired 'Is that Broadway 786?' then I would know I had to go as soon as possible to a meeting place near the pier at Weymouth. We never had occasion to use this.

When John arrived I was surprised to see that he was accompanied by his wife. After I'd greeted them and introduced them to the landlord and other acquaintances as my cousins, they explained for the benefit of all and sundry that they were touring the West Country and couldn't pass through the district without seeing cousin Harry. I hadn't seen John's wife since our introduction in the Mirabelle, and we spent a pleasant couple of hours in the pub. John made quite an impression on a farmer acquaintance of mine, who told me later that my cousin was 'very interested in farming and seemed to know quite a bit about it'. I wonder what Harold Weedon of Tatton Farm would have thought if he'd been aware that he was talking and drinking with a Russian spy—and whether he still remembers that encounter?

John had a very retentive memory. Whilst appearing to be engrossed in farming matters and discussing them so intelligently, he was at the same time 'tuned in' to what was being said by a noisy handful of youngish naval officers from the local submarine flotilla. They were chattering about a recent exercise from which they had returned that day: no uncommon occurrence, as it was their habit on returning to harbour to tank up with duty-free gin aboard ship and then come ashore to this pub, hog the bar over halves of bitter, and break every rule in the Official Secrets Act by bellowing in public the details of the anti-submarine exercises in which they had been participating.

When we left, John and his wife followed me in their car to the cottage and, after switching on the radio in the prescribed way, I did bacon and eggs for supper. While I was cooking, John sat at my bureau and made notes of the conversation he had overheard, sending his wife to me from time to time for an interpretation of naval slang he didn't understand. Over supper it transpired that they were in Dorset for the express purpose of looking at the tank ranges. In answer to my surprised recollection that a long time had gone by since Gregory mentioned the subject to me in Austria, John said the ranges had been under surveillance for a considerable period, though it was the first time he personally had been on this particular job: they worked on the basis that it was unwise for the same faces to be seen in the neighbourhood too often. I asked why they had broken the agreement that their car should not be brought to my cottage. John said it was a car hired for their 'holiday', and there was no risk, as they couldn't be traced owing to the way in which it had been hired.

I wasn't asked to do anything for them. They had contacted me and shown themselves in my company so that they would be taken for granted in the district if they had to come again. John maintained that it wasn't a bad thing to get to know local farmers and other folk—and so much the better if sponsored by a local resident.

There was certainly no cloak-and-dagger stuff when they went to Bovington. Lawrence of Arabia's cottage at Clouds Hill provided an ideal excuse in the unlikely event of their being questioned about loitering in the vicinity of the Army camp. They invited me to have a meal with them at the Seven Stars near Wool, where I think they said they were staying, but I had to decline and left them to whatever it was they had come for.

And now, soon after my return to the cottage, I was to meet a newcomer.

Nikki had vanished from the scene. It was Roman himself who summoned me to a meeting opposite the Maypole pub in Ditton Road at 5.30-pm one Saturday. I was there well ahead of time, and saw Roman drive by in the company of another man. Right on the dot I saw him again—alone. We drove in my car to a nearby sports ground, where he asked what my plans were for the evening and then asked me to go to the corner of Edgware Road and Oxford Street at 9-pm, holding a newspaper in my left hand and my glove in my right. I would be accosted by a man who would ask me if I knew what number bus went to (I think) Swiss Cottage. I would reply along the lines that I wasn't sure but thought it was probably a 37 or 39, and then he'd say, 'Are you sure it's not a 48?' or words to that effect—the passage of time has dimmed my memory as to the exact phrasing. The man who spoke would, said Roman, be the one I'd be meeting next time, and we were to make our own arrangements accordingly.

I was there on time, waiting outside a cinema on the corner. A thickset, swarthy man with smiling eyes and a wide grin came up and spoke to me, and we went through the incantation of bus numbers. He had what I took to be an American accent, though once we got talking I was to learn that he had acquired it in Canada. His name—or, at any rate, the name bestowed on him by the folk for whom he worked—was Gordon Lonsdale.

Since my release from prison it has been reported that Gordon has died. This news came as a great shock. Its only redeeming feature is that he didn't die alone and friendless in a foreign jail, which he almost certainly would have done if he hadn't been exchanged for the self-confessed British agent Greville Wynne. I'm glad he lived long enough to spend a few years at last with Galisha, the wife to whom he was passionately devoted, and his children.

Up to the time of our arrests a deep bond of friendship existed between us. I liked him at that first meeting, and the affection increased as we travelled hundreds of miles together visiting Devonport, Portsmouth, Portsdown and Barrow trying to get some gen on the *Dreadnought* during her construction, and to Bath.

There's one aspect about this whole operation which is very difficult to put into words, but which I do think needs saying. A lot of people may hate my guts. Others, more tolerant, may still find it hard to understand how I could have been drawn into such activities and carried them on for so long. What's it like, day after day, leading what can accurately be described as a double life? How can you bear the deceits, the evasions, the very job of espionage itself?

However incredible it may seem to the detached observer, there was a real camaraderie between us. All of us. I went in unwillingly, under duress; but I came to enjoy the company of the people I worked with, and the challenges they set. We were a team. The fact that I was involved with enemy agents didn't stop a real enthusiasm building up at times—not political, ideological or what have you, but just the sheer exhilaration (even when it was frightening) of getting a scarifying job done in the face of awful risks. If we had done the same sort of thing in a wartime Resistance movement, that comradeship would have been regarded as a courageous, noble thing, and we'd have been lauded as heroes. The fact that I was working for the wrong side—and I don't deny it was the wrong side, and I've paid the price for it—didn't take away from the feeling of comradeship, of being in a tense situation together and enjoying even the riskiest moments together. It ceased to be a matter of what I was doing and what its ultimate object was: it became a matter of skill and nerve, of *having* to do the job and do it without a hitch.

I'm not making excuses here. I'm just remembering what it was like.

At that first meeting with Gordon Lonsdale I suggested we went over the road into Hyde Park to talk, but this didn't appeal to him. He preferred the idea of a good supper in the Lotus House Chinese Restaurant a little further up Edgware Road. We managed a quiet table to ourselves and had a meal and a bottle of wine—of which Gordon, in accordance with what I was to find out was his custom, just toyed with one glass.

For the larger part of the time he trotted out some entertaining anecdotes about his life in Canada. Right away I saw how fond he was of 'shooting a line', but for all that there was something immediately attractive about him: it was all done with such boyish zest.

It was quite some time before odd remarks and hints began to sketch in a different personality behind the name and features of this man whose name wasn't Lonsdale and who wasn't a Canadian. Only when we had got to know each other really well and to relax in each other's company did he tell me the things he had kept hidden from business acquaintances for years, and which came as such a revelation at the trial.

The identity he had assumed was that of Gordon Arthur Lonsdale who was born on 27th August 1924 at Cobalt in Ontario. The father was a native-born Canadian who is said by some to have been a miner, by others a lumberjack. He was reported to be still living in the region, working as a handyman, in 1961. Not a lot is known about the boy's Finnish mother except that her maiden name was Bousu and that she eventually left her husband to go and live some fifty or sixty miles away in the mining town of Kirkland Lake. Here she met a Finn named Philaja, and it was under the name of Gordon Philaja that the boy went to school there. When he was eight, his mother took him with her on a trip to Finland—when all trace of the two of them was lost.

What happened to the real Gordon Lonsdale can never be known for certain. But Gordon—I have to call him this, and will always think of him as Gordon, even knowing it wasn't his real name—did once tell me: 'He was one of those who came over to us when we occupied Finland. He was on the Mannerheim Line at the time. I was put with him, and he told me what he could remember of his childhood in Canada before he left. He used his mother's name, and was killed at Stalingrad.' This may or may not be the truth: I can only set it down without comment.

Certainly the Russians helped themselves to this young man's identity. Great care was taken in the creation and training of a substitute Gordon Lonsdale. He was sent to his supposed birthplace to familiarise himself with the surroundings, to obtain a copy of his birth certificate and a passport in that name, and to live the life of Gordon Lonsdale. In Court he came unstuck on a simple matter which only someone psychic would have thought to check. The prosecution proved conclusively that he was not the person he professed to be by producing a sworn affidavit from the doctor who had attended the birth of the real Gordon. According to his case records for 1924, he had circumcised the boy. The man arrested under the name of Lonsdale had not been circumcised. It's a fair bet that future Russian spies chosen to impersonate other men will have a stricter medical examination and that certain specific matters will be checked and double-checked.

Towards the end of that first meeting we got down to some matter-of-fact arrangements. He had never been to Weymouth or Portland, and asked if our first meeting in the area could be at my cottage. I saw no objection to this, and it was all fixed.

On the appointed day I met him at Dorchester station and drove him to my home. He worked well into the night in the bathroom, photographing books and documents which I had amassed for his visit. His real intention in coming down to Weymouth, however, was to look round Portland and, he said, get the feel of the place. Before we turned in he asked if we could set out at nine o'clock in the morning for this.

I spent that morning showing him as much of Portland as could be seen from the car. The others had already done this Cook's Tour with me, and had also been round quite a lot on foot. I've often thought I had all the qualifications to set up as a one-man Portland Tourist Bureau.

There is another Admiralty establishment at Southwell on Portland, and right away Gordon talked about enlisting someone from there into our group. I utterly refused to make any approaches to anyone. He did his best to persuade me, but I got round it in the end by saying that there was no-one I knew well enough in the place.

He was dumbfounded by the dockyard itself and the obvious ease with which one could get into it.

'That security fence!' I can still hear the echo of his disbelief. 'It's just a laugh!'

As later events will show, it was just that.

Satisfied with his visit, he declared himself ready to go back to London, so I drove him to Dorchester and left him there to catch his train.

I hadn't been at all keen on touring Portland with him that day, as I'd told Bunty I simply had to go to London to see some friends and wouldn't be able to meet her until 6-pm on the Sunday. If she'd seen my car touring around, it would have involved some difficult explanations. However, when we met I discovered she hadn't been out of doors all day.

I've said that I enjoyed Gordon Lonsdale's company, and grew to enjoy it more and more. But I was also growing to enjoy Bunty's company more and more. This was where the double life grew doubly tricky. Gordon was very forceful and wanted a lot out of me. My company was suddenly much more in demand than it had been so far.

Gordon and Roman were keen to see for themselves the precise situations of Naval Establishments in various towns and cities all over the country. My brains were picked relentlessly as I plotted the places on town maps and charts—and, not content with establishing the map references, the two of them were always demanding to see the actual places. We couldn't get into the Naval Dockyards —except for one occasion when our plans to raid the Underwater Detection Establishment came at last to fruition—or into the Empire Hotel or Warminster Road buildings in Bath, then being used as Admiralty offices; but they doggedly insisted on seeing them. They were like entranced film fans outside an Odeon during a gala première, longing to get at Elizabeth Taylor but making do with a view of the outside of the building.

I drew the line when they wanted me to act as their guide inside Portsmouth Dockyard and Portland Naval Base during Navy Open Days. I know they paid their money and went in on their own from time to time, but I wasn't going to accompany them at any price: it would have been thought pretty peculiar if I'd been observed paying money to go into my regular place of employment, or for that matter anywhere else around the dockyards where I could and frequently did go during the course of my job.

By the time Gordon and Roman had finished, there wasn't an inch of the outside of the Admiralty Signal and Radar Establishment on the top of Portsdown Hill near Portsmouth that they didn't know. Wherever one could walk, they walked. I'm sure that Soviet Intelligence archives received during that period more photographs than could possibly be filed and catalogued before becoming obsolete. Although all facets of the Portland Naval Base were clearly delineated on the Admiralty charts they had bought, they nevertheless spent hours on high ground with concealed cameras taking photographs. At Southwell the Admiralty Gunnery Establishment, as it was then known, also came under their cameras, and a favourite excursion was a boat trip inside Portland Harbour to study and photograph the Naval installations from the seaward side.

Gordon was a dedicated and intelligent man, well versed in Intelligence procedures; but, as I've mentioned, somewhere along the line his superiors slipped up in putting him to work on essentially Naval matters. He was as bad as Nikki. Roman and John were first-rate, but everything had to be spelt out to the other two. On the other hand, both Nikki and Gordon had a wide knowledge of aircraft and would have done brilliantly in the Royal Observer Corps. This confirms in a roundabout way what I had come to believe about this corner of the operation: the Soviet Government wouldn't have deployed such a number of men, and men of such different expertise, in the field simply for the information they were likely to glean from me.

I more than once warned Gordon he was living on borrowed time. He ought to have a rest from the tension he was living under, otherwise a toll would be taken later. Even when he looked most at ease his mind was quiveringly alert. For example, one Sunday morning he was sitting by the fireplace of my cottage apparently without a care in the world—and for some reason I remember clearly that he was listening to a record of the Bruch Violin Concerto which he had brought me—when suddenly, for no apparent reason, he doubled up, head down, and propelled himself like a ball of lightning from his easy chair into the corner. I couldn't see any cause for this, and was taken aback.

'Who is it?' he enquired in a low voice.

He had seen passing the window, where I had not, the shadow of the man delivering the Sunday papers. I realised more than ever how he was living on his nerves. For all his warmth and good-fellowship he would never be able to relax in the exacting job he had chosen—or had thrust upon him.

I commented that for his health's sake he ought to go back to his own country. He wryly agreed, like a soldier told that the best thing for his insomnia would be to get out of the firing line, but said he wanted to manage another couple of years: he had already clocked up a good pension, but by hanging on a bit longer he would be very well off indeed. It would be worth the extra spell.

In spite of the Canadian personality and background he had soaked up, he was Russian and made no pretence otherwise with me. He often entertained me with stories of Russian folklore—and, I have to confess, equally often went on for hours without repeating himself until it dawned on him that I was ceasing to be entertained, when he would switch the subject and discourse about his wife and family.

I have every reason to believe he was brought up in China and had been there again since his marriage. He would have been a boy between the ages of three and six during the time I was in China myself, from 1927 to 1930. The average adult can usually recall certain events and moods when the right memory is triggered off, and several things Gordon related about his childhood certainly rang true to me and bore out his story that he had spent some of his early years in Nanking, Shanghai and later Peking. He had ambitions of returning to China one day—this was before China's break with Russia—and while in London he attended the School of Oriental and African Studies to keep in touch and to brush up his largely forgotten Chinese language.

During the trial a letter intended for his wife was produced and read in Court. Part of it went as follows:

> I understand you quite well. You wrote that seven October Anniversaries were celebrated without me. That is so of course. But I have celebrated them without you and without the children and my people. When we were in P, I tried to explain everything to you.

Several commentators have taken the P to stand for Prague, because in a letter from his wife, Galisha, she wrote:

> On November 3rd we had an evening party at the place

where I work and I sang, it reminded me of our life in Prague and I felt very sad.

This certainly indicates that at some stage they lived and worked in Prague, but doesn't necessarily mean that Gordon's letter refers to the same period. After many conversations with him I'm still convinced that the P in his case refers to Peking. One of his boys spoke Chinese quite well, his wife worked there at one time, and I know he joined her there for one of his leaves.

Who was he, really?

Just how intimate he was with the Krogers I can't honestly say, since he never mentioned them by name and I didn't meet them until we appeared together in the dock. Apart from them and perhaps a couple of his closest Russian colleagues, I do think I knew him better than anyone else in England. With me he didn't have to act a part. I knew him for what he was, and of course he knew I did, so he could be quite natural in his conversation with me. With anyone outside his profession he had to live a lie, and in playing a complex part he had to be consistent within it at all times. He admitted this was a strain.

He was fond of good wine and claimed to be a connoisseur of the wines of his own country, but when working he steered clear of alcohol: I never knew him permit himself more than two glasses of anything, even on occasions when we were meeting on fairly relaxed terms. 'Don't order wine,' I'd say when we were dining together, after I'd realised the discipline he imposed on himself. But he invariably ordered a full bottle and left me to dispose of most of it.

I remember him ordering a Coke in my local pub, which didn't stock it. Later the landlord asked who my companion had been, and I explained him away as a Blue Nose from Newfoundland who I'd met during the war. There was so much gossip circulating in that pub that it was a bit silly to have taken him there in the first place, with that Canadian accent of his. Nobody ever left the bar without speculation and derision starting up almost before the door had closed. Rural England! If I heard the story once, I heard it a hundred times—of the wife of the local coal merchant (well, that's what we'll say here, so they can't be identified) who got pregnant during the war and had to hare off to Wales where her boy friend, as he then was, was serving in the Army so they could get married... just in time. Or what one of the local farmers got up to on market days in Dorchester. How everyone got to know after a couple had left that they'd never been married. Almost every word I uttered in that pub, and hundreds that I didn't, later reached the Press. If they had known that my companion one evening had been the so-called 'Master Spy', this would by now have been romanticised beyond all measure.

Even in the chilliest weather Gordon never wore an overcoat. A light mac was all I ever saw him wear, and although to my knowledge he hadn't been back to Canada or the United States for some years he regularly wore the thin Dacron suit he'd brought over with him. I once asked why he didn't put on something warmer, and he simply shrugged:

'Call this weather cold? You don't know what cold *is*, in this country.'

The Press gave him the reputation of being a ladies' man, but this is very far from the truth. He certainly had a number of female friends, but he told me in my cottage one evening, when we were on the subject of women, that having intercourse with any of them was definitely out. He had been absolutely faithful to Galisha. He was inclined to shoot a line in all other respects, and I think that if he'd made any bedroom conquests he wouldn't have been able to resist boasting about these, too. Knowing him as I did, I'm positive that in this respect he had high moral standards. He was comparatively young, he was working under dangerous conditions in a foreign land, he could hardly have been blamed for seeking some physical diversions; but when I put this to him, he retorted that he'd promised Galisha to be faithful to her and he had never been known to go back on his word, least of all to his wife. He made up for lost time on leave: it was much better to return to her as he had left her. Any potentially amorous adventures that brewed up always stopped at the bedroom door. I'd have liked to tell his widow of this conversation, but of course will never get the opportunity; and maybe she doesn't need telling, anyway.

A question I put in a few different ways at different times was whether, in view of the years he had lived in the West, he would ever contemplate getting his wife and family out of Russia if that were possible and settling here or in the States, or perhaps Canada. He was always most emphatic that even if he had enough money to do this and could overcome all the snags, he wouldn't consider it. 'What has the West got to offer that Russia hasn't?' He didn't deny there was a shortage of consumer goods in the Soviet Union, but was convinced this would eventually be put right. Some articles of food were in short supply: this, too, would soon be dealt with. Present-day Russia was a comparatively new country which had started almost from scratch at the end of the old Czarist days with an Exchequer emptied by the ravages of the First World War. Now it was emerging as a powerful, wealthy country. Taxes in Russia were low, he said, Social Security benefits good, retirement benefits the best in the world. Rents weren't a major factor in household budgeting, being so cheap. I couldn't help asking about the shortage of living accommodation, cheap as that accommodation might be. This was common to most war-stricken countries, he answered, but was rapidly being overcome—and as to that, what about the shortage of housing in England and especially in London? He asked if I'd ever seen the hovels many New York workers live in—and New York didn't have the excuse of having been ravaged by an enemy.

He had impressive answers to nearly every question I raised. I'm not saying I agreed with all or any of those answers, but there was no doubt of his sincerity. Russia had the Arts, Music, Ballet, Literature...Sport in abundance. The Russian Ballet performed at prices that even the poorest could afford, and it wasn't an expensive evening out to go and hear some of the finest symphony orchestras and soloists in the world.

There was just one question with which I needled him, to which I never got a satisfactory answer. Why, in view of these other views he had expressed, did he spend up to £5 a week, using an accommodation address, doing the Pools in the hope of winning thousands of pounds?

He said it would be nice to have a large sum to draw on if he needed something which couldn't be obtained in Russia. That seemed a bit vague to me. I often wonder what might conceivably have happened if he had won £50,000 or so. Would he have stayed *then*? I think not, but one can never predict what riches will do.

One thing he felt very keenly. Neither he nor Roman, or for that matter any of the others working in this country, were connected with the Russian Embassy or any of its offshoots. An ejection of great numbers of Embassy and Trade Delegation staff such as happened late in 1971 wouldn't have made the slightest difference to the functioning of the group. I don't know whether it made any difference in 1971. I do know that contact with the Embassy was utterly forbidden in my time. Gordon used to go near it occasionally. He regarded it as a tiny patch of his homeland and longed to go in:

but they wouldn't have known who on earth he was, and his superiors back home would have been furious. The whole thing was organised throughout to avoid any embarrassing involvement of diplomats.

As I've made clear, Gordon was a real eager beaver, always on the go, making increasing demands on my time and spending a great deal of time in my company. It was growing more and more difficult to explain things to Bunty.

Sooner or later she and Gordon Lonsdale had to meet.

Chapter Eight

Microdot to Moscow

Some writers and legal loudmouths who seem to know more about the behaviour of Bunty and myself than we ourselves ever knew have declared that Bunty worked with me over a long period and knew precisely what it was all about. They also say it's nonsense to think that she didn't know who Lonsdale was. They are wrong. Quite wrong. Gordon came on the scene, so far as I was concerned, in 1960, and it was not until July of that year that I introduced him to Bunty—and then not under the name of Gordon Lonsdale.

Now that we were as good as engaged, she had for some time been growing increasingly curious—not surprisingly—about my intermittent weekend dashes up to London. Why couldn't she come as well? I told Gordon that things were getting a bit sticky, and he dreamed up a story which would cover these errands of mine. I was to describe him to Bunty as a close friend from Warsaw days, when I'd known him as Assistant Naval Attaché in the United States Embassy. So far so good. But she was still a bit dubious about this reunion of old buddies, and didn't quite see why it had to occupy so much of my time. To make it real and solid, my old friend had to show himself in person.

So I took Bunty up to London with me one weekend, with the promise that this friend had been able to get us a couple of tickets for the Bolshoi Ballet, which indeed he handed over when we met. I introduced him as Commander Alec Johnson. From that moment until our arrest, not so very far from that same meeting-place, Bunty knew Gordon only as Alec Johnson, and really believed he still served with the US Navy. In Court she was accused of acting 'for greed'—but in fact she never received a penny either from Gordon or from me.

Although Bunty was—and is—a rather shy, reserved person, not at ease when meeting strangers and preferring a quiet, withdrawn life, she began to enjoy Gordon's company as much as I did.

Then I realised where we were heading. My heart sank. Gordon, alert as ever, visualising everything and every person in terms of his task, wanted Bunty to supply information. She worked inside the Establishment, she must be of *some* use. I tried to talk him out of it, but once he got a notion in his head there was no stopping him. Surely she had access to potentially valuable information? Surely there was a way of getting his hands on some of it?

I won't say he turned ugly, but he certainly put the pressure on.

Part of Bunty's job was keeping a register of test pamphlets and other documents, issuing them when authorised to do so, and recording their distribution. Many plans and drawings went out without even these formalities. If you showed up in person you could pretty well help yourself off the racks. Draughtsmen frequently did so. If several copies were needed at any time, it was normal to select what you needed and cart the originals off to the duplicating office. Any factory, dockyard, contractor or sub-contractor wanting to refer to a specific drawing had only to write or telephone in, and it would be issued with a minimum of fuss. If Gordon had written in for the stuff he wanted on his business-headed notepaper, it would almost certainly have been sent to him without question, and then maybe Bunty would never have been involved in the wretched business. But he was too wary to provide a direct link with himself. He insisted on acquiring material via Bunty.

Putting on his bluff, warm American act as 'Alec Johnson', he hinted at doubts in the minds of the US authorities. Were the British making the best use of technical information supplied by the Americans? And there was supposed to be a two-way traffic in technical information: we shared ASDIC (now called SONAR) secrets, and he wasn't at all sure we were playing straight and passing everything over as we should. From casual hints and some sly digs which made Bunty indignant on behalf of her own Department, he went on to suggest that, just to set the minds of our Allies at rest, Bunty might confidentially let him see some test pamphlets without his having to go through official channels. That way he'd be more likely to learn the truth.

Bunty jibbed, but he was very persuasive. She expected me to second her objections, but of course I had no option but to back up Gordon.

Bunty was conned, and I was largely to blame. She went along with me because she trusted me. Looking back, it's not a savoury story, and from this distance of time it hardly seems real to either of us any more. But that's the way it was.

She helped herself to pamphlets and passed them to me. Some

went straight to Gordon. Others, which had to be returned as quickly as possible, I photographed and passed on the copies.

We had one windfall which had nothing to do with Bunty, though later there was an attempt to pin the blame on her. The Security Officer said on oath that he knew *'by sight* the defendant Gee', who had, so far as he was aware, access to test pamphlets. He agreed that she would not have had access to drawings of the atomic submarine HMS *Dreadnought* unless there had been an error in distribution, or—and this remark baffles me as much today as it did then—unless 'by reason of her employment she could have gained access to them if she had been so minded'. To which anyone in the Department could only ask, bewildered... *How?*

In fact there had been an error in distribution, but not in Bunty's direction. In my job in the Port Auxiliary Repair Unit I received all incoming correspondence and was responsible for its distribution. One day a drawing of the *Dreadnought*, correctly addressed to UDE, reached my office by mistake. Since nobody even knew it was there, it was a simple matter for me to take it home, photograph it, and send it on to its correct destination when I had finished.

What happened to all these labours of mine: what, after Gordon Lonsdale, was the next stage along the route?

As I've said, during the entire operation I never knew the Krogers by name. We never met and I was given no details of their background or where they were stationed. When the whole truth at last came out, I was as interested as anybody else in the courtroom.

The couple served Russia under a number of aliases, but their real name was Cohen. Morris Cohen was born in New York, son of Russian immigrants. For quite genuine ideological reasons his sympathies inclined to the Left. He fought against Franco in the Spanish Civil War, returned to work for a Russian company in New York, married a Polish girl, fought in the US Army during the Second World War, and afterwards became a teacher. By now he and his wife had for a long time been committed Communists. They were deeply involved with the Rosenbergs, who were charged with espionage in 1950 and executed in 1953, and after the arrest of these friends they thought it wiser not to hang around too long. In 1950 they left America. Nothing has been satisfactorily established about their activities during the next five years. It is known that they spent some time in Australia—doing what?—and were in Vienna in 1954. Then in 1955 they arrived in London, complete with forged Canadian and New Zealand passports in addition to perfectly valid American ones, and a blank British passport ready to be filled in if needed. Whenever the Cohens needed to move on, they had a fine selection of documentation to choose from.

But they were no longer the Cohens. They had become Peter and Helen Kroger.

Peter Kroger leased a room almost opposite the Law Courts and set up as an antiquarian bookseller. Within a year he had bought a pleasant bungalow at Ruislip, which served as business premises as well as home. It was also to serve in due course as a radio transmitting and receiving station.

A great many parcels moved in and out of the country. Kroger was quite genuinely interested in books, and was soon greatly respected by colleagues and contacts in the trade. He and his wife made many trips to the Continent. And he sent consignments of rare and specialised books all over the world, and received many back.

In quite a few of these books travelled microdot reductions of all the information he was being given to pass on to the Russians. He had all the equipment for this kind of work in the bungalow. To it was added radio apparatus which made direct contact possible, equipped with a keying device to send even the longest message in a swift, indecipherable burst lasting no more than a few seconds. Even if some detector did by a wild fluke pick up the transmission, its duration would be so short as to defy even the most sophisticated location equipment.

It was a complicated way of doing things. Procedures would have been much simpler for everyone if it had been possible to use the Diplomatic Bag for messages and photographs, or the Embassy radio, or even the facilities provided for trade missions visiting this country. Roman, John and Gordon all described to me at one time and another the laborious business of reducing photographs of drawings and documents to microdot form. Although they didn't exactly complain, they all thought a lot of time could have been saved by simply sending away the original films in the Diplomatic Bag. But because of embarrassment caused by accusations of spying against Embassy attachés and their staff, the chain of communication had now been rigidly laid down to exclude the Embassy altogether.

At one stage it was planned that I should be trained to make the microdots myself and pass them on through the post or by other means, thus obviating any risk of our being picked up together with incriminating evidence in our possession. I resisted this—which I regret now, in view of what happened, though really I didn't have the facilities in my cottage. However, I was supplied with a cheap microscope to enable me to read and digest any instructions which might be too complicated to remember if given verbally. This microscope had to be kept hidden, as I'd have had difficulty explaining it away should anyone visiting or staying with me have stumbled on it. Wrapped in a polythene bag and then put into a box, it probably reposes to this day just under the soil of a field, close to the hedge, not far from where I once lived.

When the microdots were passed to me they were hidden in the barrel of a Parker 51 pen or the snuffer cap of a Ronson or Dunhill lighter, which we exchanged for similar models when handing over. It was lucky that nothing had been passed on the day of our arrests, as I was carrying both lighters and the pen in my pocket at the time. When they were restored to me later it was obvious that they had been stripped and thoroughly examined by Special Branch.

Chapter Nine

Breaking In

Earlier in these pages I described a lakeside meeting near the A3. The purpose of this was to finalise the plans for the break-in at the Underwater Detection Establishment which I had discussed with the Number One man in Dublin, who had presumably given our group the go-ahead.

The night watchman had a series of clocking points to visit during the night, and my first task was to obtain a record of his rounds. It was easy enough to borrow these clock records and replace them as convenient, and I drew up a schedule of the watchman's rounds. This had to be memorised so that when members of the group met we'd be carrying nothing of an incriminating nature. It was agreed, as I'd suggested in Ireland, that the break-in should be timed for 10 pm during the watchman's supper break.

The next question concerned the keys. I made the point that as we had chosen 10 pm for the raid, the watchman would be having his supper in the room where the keyboard was situated. I rejected Roman's proposal that the man should be overpowered, and reminded them all that I had previously been assured that no violence would be used. If they didn't intend to honour this assurance, they could count me out. I knew all the watchmen, and although I didn't know who would be on duty that particular night I wasn't going to be a party to any rough stuff. In any case, we didn't want to draw attention to the fact that we'd been there, and draw the watchdogs from every little Security office on to our scent.

I suggested that the man Roman had taken with him to board the *Decibel* in Poole harbour should join the party, to which they somewhat reluctantly agreed. This reluctance changed when I told them there would be steel chests and perhaps a couple of safes to be opened if they wanted more than just a night stroll round the Establishment. I could produce duplicate keys of filing cabinets, but nothing else. It had always been a sore point with me that the duplicate keys of those cabinets were kept in the office in which I worked instead of in the Security Officer's custody, where they rightly belonged: he had little enough to do, and I resented being lumbered with even part of his job. But now this was turning out to our advantage. I promise to have certain of these duplicate keys with me on the great night.

The others were to travel down to Dorset independently. After a verbal rehearsal of the project it was decided that as we were calling in the London lock-picker to help with doors and chests, one of the rest of us ought to drop out. Obviously it couldn't be me. For reasons known only to themselves Roman said it was more important for the future that John and Gordon should go: he would withdraw. By his reference to the future I took him to mean that he would probably be the first to go back to Russia, leaving John and Gordon in England.

More details were thrashed out before Gordon and I resumed our casual stroll round the lake, and Roman and John continued with their fishing. Moorhens and mallard were swimming on the lake, and I even noticed a kingfisher. War and espionage and potential destruction seemed a hundred light years away from that tranquil spot.

The raid was planned for the following Friday evening. It was the longest wait of my life, up till that time. When I had theorised about it in Dublin and at the lakeside it had seemed a piece of cake, but now that it was actually scheduled to take place I began to anticipate all kinds of snags and last-minute mishaps. By the time we assembled in the little-used railway sidings on Portland I was in a high state of tension, which I did my best to conceal from the others. Maybe they felt the same.

It had been decided that we should wear rubber shoes for the venture. The others wore haversacks as well. I was given a pair of silken gloves and a face mask from John's haversack.

In accordance with our programme, John and the hired cracksman followed the lower railway line whilst Gordon and I went in my car to the top of Portland, where we parked in a secluded spot near the Borstal, went down the hill past HMS *Osprey*, the Anti-Submarine School, and got to the railway line by the route I had already mapped out. The object was to meet at the railway bridge crossing the Dockyard at a point close to the UDE and climb down a ladder into the Dockyard on the UDE side. We had split up into two parties at the outset as there was less chance of being seen that way. The only danger at the bridge was the proximity of half a dozen Police Quarters, though the chance of anyone entering or leaving them at the critical moment was remote.

Gordon and I reached the bridge in advance of the other two, who had farther to walk, but we were all assembled a few minutes before the scheduled time. We donned our masks, put on our gloves, and I personally secured the ladder, of extremely light rope—or maybe it was nylon—to the parapet of the bridge. As guide to the party, I was first down it. The others quickly followed, and within minutes we were at the door of our goal. It didn't take the cracksman long to open up, and while the others waited I slid quietly along to see what the watchman was doing. I could safely have predicted the position he'd be in: leaning back in a chair with his feet on the table, reading a book, with a cup of tea poured out ready for drinking. He wouldn't bother us.

A complete tour of the Establishment was made. Many flashlight photographs of objects and drawings were taken. I'm not going to run smack into the Official Secrets Act again, at my time of life, by describing in detail the nature of the material; but I do feel that if John and Gordon had gone in with a specific object in view rather than just a recce, they would have been highly successful. The man they had brought with them encountered little difficulty in opening steel chests and one safe. There was another safe he couldn't open in the time at his disposal, but having seen the make he said that if he came again he'd be able to bring something which would simplify entry. Flashlight photographs of the contents were made. Although I had the duplicate keys of certain filing cabinets in my pocket, I wasn't asked to use them.

After a good look round the establishment by the light of powerful torches, we replaced everything exactly as we had found it and let ourselves out again, locking the door and hastening to the ladder. During all that time, just over an hour and a quarter, the others had seen no-one, and I'd had only a quick glimpse of the watchman taking his ease.

We got back to the railway bridge, found the ladder undisturbed, and got up it as quickly as possible and off Admiralty property. John and his companion retraced their way back to the railway sidings, Gordon stowed the ladder away in his haversack, and we made the tedious climb back to the car.

I was asked to drive the three of them to a car park in Weymouth, they having come from there to Portland by bus. Fortunately there was no road block for an escaped prisoner this time on our way to the mainland. It has since occurred to me to wonder whether, if there had been a block, the bod we had with us from London would have been known by the warders inspecting the car. A man following his profession would almost certainly have spent some time inside.

When we arrived in Weymouth, Gordon drove the cracksman off in his car, while John chatted for a while with me and then left in his own car.

So ended their look round the Underwater Detection Establishment, which had proved, after all, to be a piece of cake. Still, I couldn't get home fast enough to down a couple of Scotches, which I considered I had fully earned.

Later I was told that one object of the exercise had been for them to find out for themselves just what the problems of getting into the Establishment were, so that they could ascertain exactly where things could be found in the event of inside help ceasing to be available at any time—which I took to mean me!

Gordon told me that 'Tony' wanted me to see someone ashore again at Church Ope Cove. I couldn't understand this after Tony's insistence that the road block risk was too great for a landing ever to be contemplated there again. We had been forced to discard another suitable spot at Osmington Mills for the same reason.

From the way Gordon was talking it was evident that he wasn't fully in the picture as to what had transpired at that Dublin meeting. The only thing I was sure of was that he was in communication with Tony, but I got the impression that he didn't actually see him in person. I passed back the message that I wouldn't be prepared to go to Church Ope Cove again, but was willing to do my part in a landing at Lulworth Cove, as discussed in Dublin. I made the further point that it would no longer be so easy for me to place landing lights at Church Ope Cove undetected. While I had been living on Portland in my caravan I could move about the neighbourhood quite freely without attracting any attention, but now that I was back in my Weymouth cottage I might arouse some curiosity if I were seen prowling around Portland late at night.

Gordon said arrangements had gone too far for them to be cancelled at this stage. I said he'd better get someone else, then. He looked amazed at this. I wasn't in too good a mood, and raged on that all this Tony was capable of doing was cracking the whip and expecting everyone to jump to it, but I wasn't going to be one of his jumpers. I had spent a lot of time with him studying charts and making plans, and now he was going back on all our arrangements without consultation.

Taken aback by this outburst, Gordon said that in the circumstances maybe Tony would want to see me himself. Would I be prepared to have another discussion with him, if necessary? That was exactly what I wanted, and I told him so.

There was no meeting in the lay-by on the Salisbury road this time. Later in the following week Gordon came to see me unannounced—I did wonder if he wasn't getting a bit careless and neglecting our usual precautions—with a request that I should go to Dublin again this coming weekend. It wasn't possible to dash off at such short notice, so we settled for the following weekend, and after making arrangements with me for my flight from Bristol he departed on foot. He didn't say where he had left his car, but at any rate he hadn't driven it right up to my place.

Things followed a similar pattern to the last time, except that it was John who met me this time at Bristol with the air ticket.

When I booked in at the Gresham Hotel as Mr Charles Casey of Bristol, the room had been reserved for me as before. When I went downstairs for a drink, however, there was no Irish coffee lady there to entertain me.

Spot on 9 pm, the man 'Tony' came to my door, ordered drinks, and placed his portable radio against the door with the volume turned low. It was as though I had never been away.

Tony was quite affable, which wasn't what I'd expected. He apologised for bringing me all this way again, but it was important to get two people ashore in England as soon as it could conveniently be arranged. I told him I hadn't changed my mind and was ready to co-operate as soon as I got the word 'go', but it would have to be Lulworth Cove, as we had previously arranged. I stressed the likelihood of a failure if he now insisted on Church Ope Cove. He agreed that the plan worked out at our previous meeting should stand: the implications of my move to Weymouth from the caravan hadn't been fully appreciated. I asked why, after being so adamant about not using Portland again, they had reversed their policy. All he had to say about this was that my sincerity about the lack of danger in the event of being stopped at a check point had impressed him so much that he himself had recommended the use of Church Ope Cove again, and the recommendation had been approved. Now the whole thing would have to be sorted out all over again.

We once more ran through the procedure for getting the two ashore. He was satisfied by my assurances that I had been to Lulworth Cove several times since seeing him and could see no snags. The only danger I could foresee would be getting them off the vessel in which they had been taking passage and in to the Cove itself. He was quick off the mark at this: that would be *their* responsibility.

I asked when the landing was likely to take place. As soon as possible, he said, subject to weather conditions and the Army Artillery practice allowing it. I was to hold myself in readiness and to be on call at any time. It might be that there'd be no preliminary warning, so from the next Tuesday to the Friday I was to make it a necessity to be in my local at 8.45 pm, where a telephone message would inform me of the timing.

He abruptly changed the subject entirely and asked why I had never mentioned the floating laboratories belonging to UDE, moored in Portland Harbour. I made some sort of answer about thinking they were unimportant, to which he retorted that they must be important, otherwise there wouldn't have been so much money allocated to them. I realised then that the laboratories would have appeared on the copies of the Sketch Estimates which I had provided. He wanted to know far more about them than I could tell him: I'd seen them but had never actually been aboard any of them.

Then came the usual Soviet question: 'Is there an armed guard on board?'

'Only a civilian shipkeeper,' I said.

He asked innumerable questions about Portland Harbour after dark—whether it was patrolled by Police or Naval launches, whether it was forbidden for civilian craft to come in after dark, and so on. I was able to give favourable answers to all these.

Could they be boarded, so that photographs could be taken of the laboratories? I replied that there'd be little difficulty in getting on board: the main problem would be hiring a motor-boat to get to them. I don't know what he expected to find aboard the floating labs, but he was so keen that when I told him it would be impossible to hire a motor-boat anywhere too close to the region, he asked me to look around, let one of the group know the cost, and I'd be given the cash to buy one. He was so elated by the recent success of getting into the Underwater Detection Establishment and, I suppose, by memories of *Decibel* a few years back, that he thought his new target would be just as easily attainable—which in point of fact it would have been—and intended to spare no expense. Before this venture could get off the ground I was arrested, and so was Gordon, so I doubt if it ever materialised.

All of a sudden he said, 'Meeting closed,' removed his radio from the door, and rang for more drinks to be bought and for some sandwiches. After we had consumed these he said goodnight and, on leaving, added with a twinkle in his eye that he would have some Irish coffee sent in to me—which he did.

After getting back to Weymouth without incident I was naturally keyed up for what the forthcoming week might have in store. Tuesday would surely be too soon for anything to happen. Wednesday was possible, and when no summons came that night I felt it was a certainty that Thursday must be the one. I must have looked at my watch every fifteen seconds from 8.30 pm onwards; but it was not to be. With 8.45 pm come and gone, I felt utterly deflated.

Friday in the office passed very slowly. I dwelt on the fact that at our meeting in Eire we had made no arrangements for a date after that day, and assumed that if the landing wasn't going to take place that evening I'd be personally contacted somehow. I hung on at the house until the last minute, arriving at the local just after 8.30 pm, and was about to order my second drink when, to my relief, I was called to the telephone. I didn't recognise the voice, but in our code language was told the landings would take place that same night at midnight.

A vast amount of organisation must have been involved in changing the arrangements in less than a week. The ship or submarine would already have been at sea while I was at the meeting in the Gresham. Since it was unlikely that Tony would have had any means of communicating with one of his country's ships at sea, he would presumably have had to return to his base—wherever that was—and get a message off to Russia from there. Upon receipt this would have had to be passed to a Soviet Naval communications department and from there to the ship. These things take time. There must also have been an enormous amount of work on board, as the whole operation had been geared to a landing at Church Ope —charts would now need to be studied again for soundings, and tides and currents assessed.

There was no particular hurry to leave this country pub, as I had ample time to get to Lulworth; but, needing all my wits about me that evening, I curbed my alcohol intake—in fact I caused a minor sensation by leaving just before closing time, since I belonged to the clique that normally stayed on drinking after permitted hours, and from my swift departure they all concluded I must be ill.

I still had time in hand when I got to Lulworth Cove. Having inspected the proposed landing place, I drove up to Durdle Dor. I had selected this as the spot from which to give a danger signal if it proved necessary, and wanted to make sure there were no cars or other obstructions. It was quite clear, so I returned with an easy mind to the cove. There I got a bit of a shock. There was now a car close to my parking place, occupied by a couple busy snogging. To be on the safe side I moved off some distance, rather further from the cove than I had anticipated in the first instance. Leaving the car, I went down to the beach, checked that there was no-one else about, and settled down to my vigil. It was a lovely evening so far as wind and sea were concerned: in fact, conditions couldn't have been better.

Now that the landings were about to take place I felt strangely unperturbed. Probably the success of that other episode at Church Ope gave added confidence. I was not to know until weeks later, after our arrest, that at this period I was supposed to have been under constant observation by Special Branch. Many writers on the subject have paid testimony to the thoroughness of this surveillance. All I can say is that if they were watching me at that time, they weren't making a terribly good job of it.

My eyes had got used to the dark by now. I strained my ears to catch the sound of any motor that might be coming in from the seaward, but with the gentle lapping of the waves on the beach I didn't hear it until some seconds after I had already seen it. I guided it in to the landing place with my torch. History repeated itself: the boat grounded, the two passengers scrambled out, turned it round nose to sea, and it was smoothly away in the same carefully rehearsed drill as last time. I introduced myself by asking if they had caught any fish, and received the stock reply.

Whilst shaking hands and welcoming them ashore I was surprised to discover, from the voice and the small, soft hand, that one of them was a woman. We made our way to the car, and I could just discern that she was wearing slacks and had a scarf over her hair, mill-girl style. They had come ashore in Wellingtons, like their predecessors, and when we reached the car changed quickly into shoes which had been fastened round their necks. Both appeared to speak English well.

I assured them that from now on there wasn't the slightest danger, so they should relax and make themselves comfortable. Each accepted a cigarette, and we started on our journey to Ringwood. I had come prepared with plenty of cigarettes, and they chain-smoked almost all the way. Neither carried any luggage. Very little was said to me during the journey: they sat in the back of the car and talked together in low tones, and I hadn't the foggiest idea what they were saying or even what language they were using.

We hadn't travelled many miles when the man leaned forward, tapped me on the shoulder and said rather awkwardly: 'The lady urgently wants to go somewhere.'

We were just approaching Wareham, so I drove to the public convenience at the Old Granary, got a coin from my pocket, and asked if she knew how these things worked.

'But of course,' she said pleasantly in English.

The parking place outside the toilets was brightly lit, and the man said it was too bright here for her to leave the car, so we had to wait until we reached a quiet bit of road. I only put this on record because the way she said 'But of course,' when I was handing her the penny told me beyond doubt that this wasn't the first time she had been in England: so far as I know, they don't have coin-op toilets in Russia.

There were no incidents on our way to Ringwood and very little traffic on the road at that time of night. On arrival at the car park I sought out and found a car with a white patch on its windscreen as arranged. I drew up near it and waited. After an interval a man got out of the car and came over to us. It was Gordon. He asked if everything was all right, and was pleased by my assurance that there hadn't been the slightest hitch. The passengers alighted, shook hands with Gordon, collected their Wellingtons from the boot, thanked me for my help and, after bidding me farewell, left in Gordon's car in the direction of London.

I waited long enough to smoke a cigarette after they had driven off, and made my way back to Weymouth reflecting how easy it all was and how stupid I had been to worry about its success. Little did any of us realise what a narrow squeak we'd have had if Special Branch, who had Gordon and myself under suspicion, had really been on the ball: if we'd had even a notion of that, there'd have been everything to worry about.

That was the last major operation we were to carry out. There was little time for self-congratulation. Nemesis overtook us a few short weeks afterwards.

Chapter Ten

Closing In

How were we tracked down and caught, in the end?

One favourite explanation of the pundits has been the hoary old story about my drinking too much, living above my income, taking Bunty on extravagant weekends to London, and attracting the attention of policemen all over Dorset by my erratic driving.

In reality I made it a golden rule never to spend on pleasure, clothes or any sort of entertainment more than my monthly salary. Anyone interested enough to analyse my expenditure would have discovered that I finished each month with a small surplus. Too many people have been detected in the dangerous game of espionage because of spending more than their known income. I had been warned of this right from the start by my Soviet contacts.

Some lovable old friends claimed afterwards that I spent £20 a week on drink. I've no intention of disputing that I liked a drink, though as much for the sake of the company as for the stuff itself. Two or three evenings a week I went to one or other of the local pubs and drank Guinness, then at 1/6d a bottle in the best room. If I stayed after closing time, which, as I've mentioned, I often did, then—and only then—did I change to Scotch at 1/10d a nip. I can recall only three occasions when I had as much as a glass of ale at lunchtime except for the usual pre-Christmas celebrations, when many of our office and the drawing office staff went to a pub just outside the gate of the Naval Base for a drink. I always had a bottle of gin and one of Scotch in the house for visitors. But at 1960 prices, to have spent £20 a week would have turned one into an alcoholic in a very short space of time.

As a junior Civil Servant I'd have been in danger of a reprimand if I had shown any after-effects of heavy drinking. This would have been reflected in my Annual Report, which, according to regulations, would have had to be shown to me. No adverse report was in fact ever shown to me.

I wonder if Tank ever had his report waved under his nose? Tank was a member of the staff who, strictly speaking, could be regarded as a Civil Servant but who worked more closely with the Naval side of the Establishment. He owed his nickname to his capacity for swallowing gin. Being a fringe senior grade, he used the senior staff mess, which had a bar. Rather than pay bar prices he had fixed it that he should have his own bottle of gin stashed away behind the bar, to be replenished as required; and to prevent unauthorised swipes from it he made pencil marks showing the level at the end of each lunchtime session. One could never tell whether he was under the influence or not: he always looked just the same.

One evening about 7 pm his wife phoned the Establishment to inquire if Tank had left. The night watchman assured her that everyone had gone home for the night. Later, on his rounds, he went into the gents' washroom and to his amazement heard the sound of someone snoring. Banging on the door of the locked lavatory cubicle brought no response. A patrolling dockyard policeman was called in, and helped the watchman over the top of the door. He found the missing Tank fast asleep on the pan with his trousers down around his ankles. The watchman unlocked the door from the inside, and sent Tank home by taxi. Both the watchman and the patrolman were duty bound to enter this occurrence in their books, but up to the time of my arrest Tank was still carrying on as usual at UDE. Whether someone covered up for him, or whether he got a reprimand, I don't know. He died some time later.

What I do know is that *I* was never criticised for behaviour of this kind. Even if the Admiralty authorities had been inclined to trust me with a responsible job after I'd been found guilty of persistent drunkenness, which is unlikely, my Russian employers certainly wouldn't have risked it. But malicious legends die hard.

Then there was the tale of my taking Bunty on weekend sprees to London, including several at the Cumberland Hotel, where I gather I threw money about like water. The sober truth (and I do mean sober) is that Bunty stayed only once with me at the Cumberland.

The Meadow View Road cottage had been paid for from my salary and the large allowances I received while in Warsaw, together with money from the black market deals. There was therefore no rent to pay: the only outgoings were rates, which were pretty low, gas, electricity, and food. To a man in my position this meant I could enjoy many things which a lot of my colleagues with crippling mortgages round their necks or heavy rents to pay, many with growing families to feed, clothe and educate, couldn't possibly afford. I often detected a note of envy during our conversations.

As I have said, I let Peggy have the house during our separation, while I went to live in a caravan. When she wanted a divorce in order to marry someone else, I put no obstacles in her way. Once it was all cleared up, I took possession of the cottage again. I was still, however, not too hard-hearted about things. When she left I told her to take some of the furniture if it would help her to make a good start with her new husband. She took full advantage of this: when I returned there to live, she hadn't left as much as a chair for me to sit on, and for a few days I had to use a kitchen stool at mealtimes. I had to refurnish the cottage almost completely: chairs, bed, bedroom furniture, sideboard and other articles. Later, neighbours were to remark how much new furniture had been taken into the cottage; but they were oddly forgetful about the amount that had been taken out. I keep coming across references to my plushy new carpets (which I didn't have) and to my £150 radiogram (actually 69 guineas—I still have the receipt).

I might, for all these inquisitive snoopers knew, have been doing what everyone else did, and buying furniture on hire purchase, without unduly straining my resources. The fact that I paid cash was unknown to them and in any case had no sinister significance.

On top of everything, I was extremely lucky with Ernie. One morning before setting out for the office I received a letter from Lytham St Anne's notifying me that I had won £100 in the Premium Bond draw. I showed this letter to friends in the Establishment and received the expected congratulations and the equally expected envious noises of those who had held Premium Bonds for ages but whom Ernie had passed by. Imagine my surprise on returning home that evening to find another letter from Lytham St Anne's which had come by the second post: greedily hoping it might be another £100 win, I couldn't open the envelope fast enough...to find with a twinge of disappointment that I had indeed had another win in the same draw, but this time for only £25. Two wins in one day! It was only by producing the two letters that I could convince my colleagues it had really happened.

Armchair detectives have nevertheless been confident ever since that No 8 Meadow View Road was refurnished by Joe Stalin.

It won't do. My personal life and personal expenditure would never have brought me to the attention of the British Secret Police. But they certainly did, after a long time, get on our trail.

During my early months in Winchester prison, many abortive attempts were made by various inquisitors to get me to talk about what had happened prior to our arrest. During one of these interviews I was told, probably to give the impression that they knew a good deal more than they really did, that the first intimation of my activities came from a Russian or Polish defector in a statement to the US authorities. There may have been a grain of truth in this. Some confirmation appears in a series of articles in the *Saturday Evening Post* called *The Espionage Establishment* by David Wise and Thomas B. Ross. In the instalment of 4th November 1967, entitled *The Spies on Our Side*, they say:

> How had MI5 picked up their traces? Some speculated it was because Houghton was overly spending his money at local pubs. In fact it was the CIA which first learned about Houghton from Michal Goleniewski, a defector from the Polish Intelligence Service. The tip was passed on to MI5. Goleniewski was in a position to know because Houghton, while serving at the Warsaw Embassy, had either compromised himself with Polish Intelligence or had come to its attention as a likely recruit.

Of all the thousands of words written about the case, the above are about the only ones which have been verified to me by the authorities. Anything else, other than the actual evidence given at the trial, is mostly speculation.

My own feeling is that the counter-espionage campaign was triggered off by someone who had tried to draw attention to me earlier, and failed. Now she was determined to make someone listen.

I'm referring to my ex-wife.

How much she really knew or suspected, I can never know for certain. The Romer Report which emerged from the official inquiry after the case states that on one occasion she reported to my superior in the office that I was engaged in espionage. This must have been after one of our quarrels. As a rule she asked no questions and made no fuss so long as extra money kept coming her way. Whether this outburst of hers was passed on to the Security Officer, Commander Crewe-Read, I'm not quite clear. I do know that as a result of the Report the Commander was retired from his post and my superior, who in the meantime had been transferred during a departmental reshuffle, incurred the Romer Tribunal's displeasure.

He was not called at the trial, but my superior in the Port

Auxiliary Repair Unit was, and made a deposition on oath to the effect that in my job I would have access to a publication called *Particulars of War Vessels*. I won't go into the pros and cons of whether I did or did not get my hands on this—the Court decided I had done so, and that Bunty was implicated—but in view of the fact that this officer stated at the Old Bailey that the publication was kept in his safe and that he kept the key on his person, I'd still be interested to hear his own explanation of such a Houdini-like feat.

Since my release I've been told by an acquaintance that Peggy blabbed to him also that I was a Russian spy. Knowing we were on the verge of parting, he dismissed this as hysterical malice and thought no more of it until I was arrested. There was also a mechanic who, when I was back in the cottage, came to repair the radio and commented that he'd been here before, and that on his last visit my wife had informed him I was a Russian spy. He thought it was too funny for words.

These two men laughed at what they had heard. But if she had told them things like this, how many others did she tell—and how many of them failed to find it funny? Whichever way it was put, it could eventually filter back to someone whose business it was to check on such rumours.

Perhaps I ought to have been more alert to the danger. During the final stages of our break-up, when Peggy was spending most of her time with her future husband, the Dockyard Welfare Officer phoned my office one lunchtime to ask if I would go over and speak to a Mr and Mrs Moon. As the name meant nothing to me, I was a bit perplexed, but made my way across. The couple introduced themselves as sister and brother-in-law of the man Peggy was going about with, and asked what it all meant. Obviously they had their brother's interest at heart. During the course of this meeting Mrs Moon let out that Peggy was saying the most fantastic things about me. I pressed her hard to explain what these things were, but Mr Moon forbade his wife to repeat any of the statements. It seems only too likely that they, too, had been told I was a Russian spy.

I have also read—rather too late in the day—that Peggy is reported as having said, when applying for divorce papers: 'You won't believe it, but I'm sure he's spying. I thought so in Poland too. There are the parcels, and the camera—and he once told me he was only making use of Bunty Gee.'

And the Security Service woke up.

It says little for the efficiency of the Security Service or the police that Peter Kroger, an important wanted man in the States, should so easily have entered this country and set up a business almost on Scotland Yard's doorstep, although photographs and descriptions of himself and his wife had been widely circulated. Furthermore, Helen Kroger had the distinguishing feature of a wide gap between two of her front teeth. Yet she and her husband moved openly about London, and none of the plain clothes men who abound in the London streets spotted them. It was not until well into 1960 that, shadowing Gordon Lonsdale to a house in Ruislip, Special Branch had any hint about the involvement of the Krogers; and not until January of the following year, after our arrest, that application made at Bow Street Magistrates' Court for their fingerprints to be taken revealed exactly who they were.

In the opening chapter I gave a few quotations from the evidence of an agent who watched us on that July day in 1960 when Bunty met Gordon Lonsdale for the first time. The pattern of subsequent 'tailings', built up by the depositions of various anonymous agents, is an impressive one, but pitted with some remarkable holes. What is most impressive is their doggedness in following us on largely trivial errands, while missing some of the really crucial meetings.

When these members of the Secret Police appeared in Court they were allowed to give no name but to identify themselves merely by letters. In the following extracts, spelling and punctuation are as in the original transcripts of their depositions. The comments in italics are mine.

SATURDAY 9th JULY 1960
WITNESS B *(The afternoon of the day referred to above)*
    On 9th July during the earlier afternoon I'd been keeping observation on Houghton and Lonsdale in the area of the old Vic, and just before 5 pm I'd seen Houghton hand a parcel to Lonsdale in the garden opposite the Old Vic.

(This was Gordon's plastic mac.)

    At 5 pm Lonsdale left Houghton and Gee taking with him a carrier bag and the parcel that had been handed to him.
    I followed Houghton and Gee into Waterloo Station. After a

cup of tea they went to Cumberland Hotel by Underground and arrived there at 5-45 pm. At 6-45 pm I saw Houghton again in the foyer of the hotel and soon afterwards Gee joined him and they went to the Albert Hall and saw a performance of Bolshoi Ballet. They left at 9-30 pm and went to a public house in Knightsbridge. I then ceased observation at 10-30 pm.

SATURDAY 6th AUGUST 1960
WITNESS I

On Saturday August 6th 1960 I was with other officers on duty at Waterloo Station. At 3-40 pm I saw Houghton arrive on a train from Salisbury. He was alone and carrying a briefcase. He left the Station and walked into Waterloo Road and to the Old Vic Theatre and stood waiting in front. At 4 pm Lonsdale joined him there. After they'd met they walked together into Lower Marsh; at one time they paused in a shop doorway and seemed to be discussing a yellow ticket or tickets held by Lonsdale. That "yellow ticket" was approximately 2 inches by 3 inches.

*(This was a programme
for the Proms, which
I went to later, and
must have been about
6 by 4.)*

They then left the doorway. I couldn't see who had the ticket then. They continued in Lower Marsh and entered Steve's restaurant at No. 30. I waited outside. At 4-30 pm Houghton and Lonsdale left the café and walked from Lower Marsh through Oral Street—that was what I read that day but I see from the plan it was Coral Street. Then into Bayliss Road and then they went to a phone box on the South pavement at the junction of Coral Street and Bayliss Road.

There Lonsdale held the door of the kiosk open whilst Houghton entered the kiosk.

*(Funny, but I recall
this quite clearly.
Loose elastic in my
pants—went in
to adjust them.)*

Then Lonsdale held out a newspaper to Houghton who took a package from his brief case and placed it within the folded newspaper which was returned to Lonsdale, i.e. the newspaper with the package was returned to Lonsdale. The package was approx—14 inches by 3 inches by 2 inches.

(He must have had telescopic eyesight to assess these dimensions from where he was hiding.)

Then the 2 turned into the Waterloo Road and returned to the Waterloo Station area at the tunnel to the Underground booking hall entrance. Lonsdale then left Houghton and Lonsdale went into the station and was not seen again—that was at 4-40 pm.

I followed Houghton by Underground to the Cumberland Hotel and he there appeared to book himself in at the desk and took a key and presumably went to his room.

At 5-50 pm he returned to the foyer and a few minutes later he was joined by a woman. They went to the bar and I ceased observation at 6-40 pm.

(The woman was not Bunty. After a drink I left her and went alone to the Proms.)

On that same Saturday another agent, Witness D, followed Gordon and myself into Steve's Restaurant and there, as I've mentioned earlier, missed the opportunity of his lifetime. His report, in detail, runs as follows:

On Saturday 6th August 1960 at 4–10 pm I saw the defendants Lonsdale and Houghton enter Steve's Café at 30 Lower Marsh.

(Name above window in large letters was actually 'Steve's Restaurant'.)

I entered 2 or 3 minutes later and I saw Lonsdale and

Houghton sitting facing each other at a table on the left hand side furthest from the door. I and a colleague sat down at an empty table next to them. We were seated so that my back almost touched Lonsdale who was then drinking refreshment and looking at a newspaper cutting. I heard Lonsdale say "I wonder if this story is correct." Houghton replied, "Yes, I'm sure they went over." I was not able to see what the cutting was about. I heard wisps of conversation between them and I gathered they were talking about 2 U.S.A. maths experts who had defected to the U.S.S.R. I didn't hear the names mentioned. I then heard Lonsdale say "You seem to have plenty in your attache case." Houghton replied, "Yes, I've more than my sleeping and shaving kit." Lonsdale then said, "We can arrange these meetings if you would like to put them in your book." Houghton said, "Yes, they will, they will take some remembering."

(Pure invention, bearing no relation to anything we said or did.)

Lonsdale continued, "These will be the first Saturday in each month especially the first Saturday in October and November at Euston. The driver will sit in a car in the area. I don't know where. I'm 90 per cent sure I will be there. We will use an interpreter. You will have to find him."

(Utter rot. How could I have found an interpreter? And why should we have needed one, when we all spoke English?)

They then spoke together of the benefit of Houghton leaving his car at Salisbury and coming to London by train. Lonsdale then said, "The packet looks fat, seems like a lot of work for me tonight." Houghton laughed and said, "Plenty, and that room at the hotel is expensive." Lonsdale replied "That will be taken care of..."

Lonsdale kept bending his head forward and speaking in low tones. These parts of the conversation were very difficult to hear. I had to strain to hear but I did hear. Finally Houghton said just before they left, "I don't want paying yet."

(A likely story! I have never been known to decline money.)

Lonsdale had said when speaking in low tones some things which I did not hear. I have however given in evidence all the parts I did hear.

He had also given in evidence a lot of things he couldn't possibly have heard because they hadn't been said. But the most shattering thing of all was his admission, when cross-examined by Lonsdale's counsel:

'I did go to keep observation on the 5th November in the Waterloo area. I also went to the same area during the first week in January 61. I never went to Euston.'

He never went to Euston...! The only thing in his wildly inaccurate testimony which bore any resemblance to anything which was actually said on that day—and he let it slip.

The sequence of events afterwards may show why he or his superiors were foolish enough to neglect that opportunity—and also one or two other things they neglected.

FRIDAY 26th AUGUST 1960
WITNESS E

On Friday 26th August at 1-40 pm I saw Lonsdale alone in a Standard car WCV 700 driving in Craven Road towards Praed Street. I followed him and he parked the car in Great Portland Street and about 4 minutes later he returned to his car and took from it what appeared to be a brown leather brief case, a brown attaché case and a grey looking metal box—possibly a safe box.

The Exhibit 51 could have been that attaché case. He took those articles into the bank and at 2-25 pm he left without them and got into his car and drove away and I then ceased observation.

On Monday 24th October at 1-35 pm I was keeping observation in Great Portland Street and at 1-45 pm I saw Lonsdale leave the Midland Bank carrying the same articles as he'd

taken in on the 26th August. He caught a bus and travelled to
Piccadilly Circus and from there he walked to 19 Wardour
Street carrying now only the brown leather brief case. I saw
him do some shopping around that area and then he went to
Piccadilly Underground and travelled via Finchley Road to
Ruislip Manor. I followed him as he left Ruislip Manor station
and he walked along Shenley Avenue, Rosebery Vale, Cornwall
Road and then turned right from Cornwall Road into the small
private road between Nos 79 and 81. By that private road I now
know by investigation that one can gain access to the front of
No. 45 Cranley Drive.

(The Krogers' home.)

The manager of the Midland Bank in Great Portland Street also
testified. He reported of Gordon Lonsdale, who had an account
there:

> On 26th August 1960 he deposited with me for safe custody a
> brown attaché case, a brown paper parcel and a deed box.
> On 24th September Supt. Smith called upon me with a search
> warrant authorising him to seize the property of Mr. Lonsdale
> and in accordance with that I handed to Supt. Smith the
> attaché case. He took it away and on 26th September he
> returned it to me and I retained it in my custody until Lonsdale
> collected it on 24th October about 1-30 pm. Apart from Supt.
> Smith neither Lonsdale nor anyone else had had possession of
> the case between 26th August and 24th October.

For those of you who think your bank account is sacrosanct,
don't be too sure. Any Government agency which cares to apply for a
search warrant under any pretext whatsoever can have a look at the
lot.

In spite of his examination of Gordon's property, Superintendent
Smith apparently did nothing about any of the lines he could so
profitably have followed up. He waited a full month before getting
his search warrant: if he had been a bit quicker off the mark, it's
doubtful that we'd have got away with our September meeting
unobserved—though we might still have done so, since the October
meeting took place without let or hindrance, and by then he must

have been fully aware of the significance of the articles which Gordon had deposited.

I really think that with the resources at his disposal he ought to have done a bit better. He failed to catch Roman, John, the two men in the car whom I never met but to whom I've referred, and the bod I contacted in the *Bunch of Grapes* in Brompton Road.

John and Roman were to my certain knowledge in London on the first Saturday in September 1960. Gordon and I had been meeting regularly since June. In August he told me excitedly that he was going home for a spot of leave to see his wife and children. It was because of this that he deposited his typewriter and brief-case in the bank.

Which meant, thought Special Branch, wrongheadedly believing to the last that Gordon was our senior man, that the spy ring had closed down for the summer recess. A worse boob it would have been impossible to make. If they hadn't knocked off for their own summer vacation they might have got Roman and John in the net, for one of them drove the other to meet me that September Saturday at a rendezvous near Chessington Zoo.

On this occasion I gave John an envelope containing documents and films, and he asked if I'd be going on to London after our meeting. I said I planned to see a friend in town later that evening, and he asked for a lift as far as the Robin Hood Gate. When I'd agreed, he excused himself and went off, to come back a few minutes later without the envelope. Presumably its contents were on their way with Roman to the Krogers.

We had a 'business' discussion in the car, made arrangements for our next meeting, and drove off to the Robin Hood Gate. On arrival, John said he was a little early, so we had a drink together and then left the pub at 9 pm. Being curious to know who was picking him up, I made for the gents' toilet in the corner of the car park and watched him leave in a car, not the same one which he'd had on arrival at Chessington—but again driven by Roman.

The arrangement we had made was for me to meet John at the back of Selfridges the next morning, Sunday, when he would return the envelope and supply more films. After a night in London, drinking with some friends in the Players Club and then sleeping at the Victory Ex-Services Club, I picked up John and drove him round a couple of blocks to make sure we weren't being observed before I took back the envelope.

If it hadn't been taken for granted that Gordon's absence meant a lull in our activities, the Secret Police would have been able to place Roman and John under surveillance, arrest them along with us, and possibly send John's wife to join Bunty and Mrs Kroger in Holloway.

After dropping John that Sunday, I called on a friend of a friend from South Africa and then made for the A1, branching off at Stamford to spend a couple of days in Lincoln visiting relatives. I had booked into the Albion Hotel by post from Weymouth. On Tuesday 6th September I checked out and drove down to Coventry to spend the rest of that day with friends, going to see the old and new Coventry Cathedral in the afternoon. I stayed the night with these friends, returned to the cottage in Weymouth on the Wednesday, and was back in the office Thursday morning.

If anyone wishes to challenge my assertion that it was during these few days that the Secret Police missed their chance of a laurel crown, I must admit I can hardly quote at this time watertight proof of my meeting with John. But if a check is made of the Attendance Register in the Port Auxiliary Repair Unit it will show that I was absent from the office before the weekend until the Thursday; the booking sheets of the Victory Ex-Service Club will show me booked in there for 3rd September; and the Albion Hotel, Lincoln, register will show I stayed there on the Sunday and Monday nights.

Detective Superintendent George Smith of Special Branch got high commendation after the trial, and was referred to in the Press as the Spycatcher. Before the trial and in letters afterwards, we always referred to him as the Flycatcher—and even so his web was by no means sticky enough.

Our old friend Witness D, who gave such misleading evidence of what he claimed to have overheard in the café on 6th August, distinguished himself with further inventions concerning events on 5th November of that year.

At the end of his original testimony he had, on oath and under cross-examination, said:

> I did go to keep observation on the 5th November in the Waterloo area. I also went to the same area during the first week in January 61. I never went to Euston.

But the following day he stated:

When in cross-examination yesterday I said that on 5th November I kept observation in the Waterloo area that was a mistake.

I did say I was keeping observation on 5th November and I was keeping observation but at Puddletown Dorset not in Waterloo area.

Puddletown is 120 miles from Waterloo. By such witnesses as this were convictions obtained.

On that Saturday 5th November another agent, identified in Court as F, waited at the junction of the B3390 and the A35 at Puddletown until I passed, and followed me to Ringwood, where I stopped for a drink. This man was obsessed by the mysterious cardboard box on the back seat of my Renault—which was my shopping box. He trailed me into London and witnessed a meeting between Gordon and myself outside the Maypole public house in Surbiton. We drove around and then parked in a dark street while we completed our business, then went back to the Maypole for a drink. This shadow's testimony was accurate on the whole, but he went off the rails a bit while fretting over the fact that when we left the pub Gordon was

> carrying a black document case of I believe the type that zips round the top and not of the type of brief case which he'd had when he arrived. I hadn't seen what had happened to that brief case.

It sounds suitably blood-and-thunderish, put like that. In fact Gordon had had the same case with him the whole time.

Witness D, having sorted out just where he was on that date, hastened to trot out more or less the same story as his pal's:

> On Saturday, 5th November, 1960 I was on duty in an official car at Puddletown, near Weymouth. At 12.10 pm having received certain information, I was in the car with a colleague at the junction of the A35 and the B3390 and saw Houghton driving his Renault Dauphine car, Index No. XOW 513 towards London. He was alone. At 1 pm. he stopped at St. Leonard's, Ringwood, and entered the St. Leonards Public House. At 1.30 pm. he left the Public House and entered his car. He then

continued driving towards London, stopping at a toilet, Filling Station and Cafe en route...

Luck was with me that day. Besides having material in my possession for Gordon to photograph, I had one of the packages I periodically collected from the Alresford public lavatory. Mr D had seen me go in and out, and both he and Mr F saw me meet Gordon. At no stage did they intervene to stop the material on its way out of the country. The package was in my pocket from 2 pm until 8.30 pm, when I handed it over to the man in the *Bunch of Grapes*. I was observed at Alresford; I was observed as far as the door of the *Bunch of Grapes*. Yet I wasn't followed in, either into the lavatory or the pub. What chances of promotion tossed away!

Not that I'm complaining: I did have another couple of months' freedom because of it.

That same day and the following day, and regularly from then on, various agents reported the appearance of Gordon's Studebaker parked near the Krogers' house. Although it is not part of my personal story, I think one extract from a report by Witness I is of interest, showing as it does how the various bits tie in:

> On Sunday 6th November I commenced observation in Cranley Drive at 2-40 pm. At 4 pm I saw defendant Mrs Kroger drive up to 45 Cranley Drive in a Consul 998 LME. She put the car in the garage and entered the front door of the house with a key.
>
> At 4-3 pm I saw Lonsdale appear on foot from the lane which connects Willow Gardens with Cranley Drive. He walked to gate of 45, Cranley Drive and as he did so he was behaving furtively, i.e. he was looking back from whence he came. His entry through the front door was very quick and he did not appear to use a key.

Harking back to that meeting on the first Saturday in October at Euston, so blithely ignored by our pursuers, I found myself chewing over one or two problems. Gordon had mentioned that there would be a car, and as there might have been some congestion if I also turned up in a car, I decided to drive from Weymouth to Salisbury and continue to London by train. Arriving at 4 pm I found Roman himself near the station, and after checking as far as possible that we were not being observed—no mean task in the

Euston bustle—we walked a few hundred yards to his car. Roman was the driver mentioned by Gordon in the café and duly recorded by the eavesdropper.

We drove off and eventually headed north on the A1. When I queried this change of stamping ground, Roman said we had been meeting on the south side of London too frequently, and in any event he personally was more familiar with the north side. Leaving the A1, we drove down several side roads, finally drawing up near a gate into a field. We strolled in this field and conducted our business there, keeping the car in view. Roman then gave me a long discourse on the dangers of a listening device being planted in my car, or even a homing device. I shrugged this off, little dreaming that a homing device had already been placed in it: Detective Superintendent George Smith told me about this later. Roman was deadly serious, and this was probably why we used his car in preference to mine. I had noticed that he wouldn't talk very freely on our journey out, and he now gave this as the reason: he was merely carrying out basic precautions, even though he had a good idea where to look for such devices and was pretty sure his own car was clean.

By this time it was almost dark. Having settled all outstanding points, Roman drove us to a pleasant country restaurant where we had dinner. Over the meal I remarked that, apart from catching a glimpse of him a couple of times last month when he drove John to meet me, or to pick John up, I hadn't seen him for some time. What had he been doing with himself? As we were casual diners who had simply wandered in on the spur of the moment without booking, there wasn't much likelihood of the table being bugged, so he talked fairly freely when the waiter was out of earshot.

He explained that he had been home on leave. I must have looked incredulous—him, and now Gordon? He assured me that secret agents on foreign service had what we in England would call a leave entitlement. When circumstances allowed, his superiors liked their men in the field to take advantage of it. Whilst it wasn't unpleasant working in the decadent West (Roman didn't actually use the word 'decadent' but his whole manner implied it), his home, friends and heart were in Russia: he could relax there and have six weeks' absolute peace of mind. He had been to Yalta, and in view of his dangerous occupation was given an extended stay. I gathered he stayed not in the ordinary workers' hotel or hostel but in much superior accommodation. He laughed when I commented that all men are equal in Soviet countries but at Yalta some are more equal than others.

I asked if he had a car in Russia. Up to the time of his return he hadn't been allocated one. Cars manufactured in Russia were mainly exported, and of those available in Russia itself the majority went to different departments, offices and factories on a rota system, where they were drawn for: the more senior people had more chances in the draw. He also explained the method of payment through their salaries. I tried to draw him on the subject of his family, but he was very evasive. Whilst John and Gordon would talk freely about theirs, I never did learn whether or not Roman was married and, if so, whether there were any children.

After this leisurely dinner he drove me to Wembley, where I got a train to the West End. Next morning he picked me up in Seymour Street at the bottom of the Edgware Road, gave me back the documents he had photographed, and dropped me near Waterloo. I got the train to Salisbury, picked up my car, and was back in Weymouth at about 2.30 pm. This time the Secret Police were quite unaware that I had been away.

Some reader is bound to ask if we never suspected that we were being followed.

Perhaps if Gordon and I had been as careful as Roman was, we might have escaped observation. Either Roman's views on the danger of bugged cars weren't imparted to Gordon or else Gordon ignored them, as at our very next meeting the whole of our business was transacted in my car. We were getting too blasé about the whole thing, and by no means taking the defensive measures we should have done.

Not that we went blundering on, heedless of risks. We maintained the complicated system of signals and meeting-places which I've already described. Visitors' cars were never parked anywhere near my cottage. En route to a rendezvous I didn't just bash on regardless, but kept a wary eye on my driving mirror; walking, I had a good look round when approaching or turning a corner, or talking to any of my contacts.

But our pursuers had unlimited resources at their disposal. Time and money were no object. They handed on surveillance from one to another, and when following me over any considerable distance didn't stick to the same car. I've reason to believe that at about the time when I might be getting suspicious at the sight of one particular car constantly behind me, they would ditch it and pick up another from a side road or lay-by. If only I'd been able to see the face of the driver rather than the car, it might have been different: if just once I'd spotted, over several hours or even on different days, the same face coming up behind me, the whole story could have ended very differently.

It ended, in fact, on Saturday 7th January 1961.

That morning I had picked up Bunty from home and driven her to Salisbury. We had lunch and did some shopping, and then went by train to Waterloo. The romancers have declared that this was meant to be the beginning of another of those lavish weekends of ours, but in fact we had day returns and intended, after a brief meeting with Gordon to hand over some material, to come home that night. I'm afraid we didn't get home.

We were early for our appointment, so on impulse we ran for a bus heading towards Walworth, where Bunty liked to visit a colourful street market. I did have one faint flicker of a warning here. As we caught the bus I looked back to see a man racing after it, and it did occur to me to wonder what the bloke was doing, tearing along like that in such desperation. But the alarm bell didn't ring loudly enough.

We spent a little while in the market, then made our way back to our prearranged meeting-place in Lower Marsh near the Old Vic. Gordon was soon on the scene.

So was Superintendent Smith. He stepped on to the pavement in front of us, identified himself, and told us we were under arrest. Special Branch cars moved in by the kerb to collect us—complete with the shopping bag containing films and pamphlets which Gordon had just taken over.

We were soon joined in custody by the Krogers. Smith had gone straight on to arrest them, taking a bit of a chance in view of the lack of any really substantial evidence against them on any count so far. The chance paid off. Once the Krogers were out of their house it was taken apart, to reveal radio transmitter, camera, talcum tins and lighters with secret compartments, the whole James Bond collection.

But one thing they never did find. It happened to be the most important thing of all.

The ingredients collected by Special Branch were all duly recorded, and if we examine what was produced in Court we get a clear picture.

In Gordon Lonsdale's flat
In a secret cavity in a Yardley's powder tin:
A negative of a signal plan.
A print of a signal plan.
A print of another signal plan.
In a secret cavity in the wooden bowl of a Ronson lighter (this lighter having been in Smith's hands before, when deposited in Gordon's bank in the zip bag):
A print of a signal plan.
A number of red and black 'one time' pads.

In the Krogers' bungalow
In a secret cavity of a Ronson lighter:
Two identical negatives of a signal plan giving dates ranging from 14th April 1960 to 26th January 1961.
A print of a signal plan relating to the 1st and 3rd Sundays in each month.
A signal plan relating to Mondays in each month.
A signal plan with columns headed in Russian.

Plus, of course, the necessary listening devices, numbered accessories, and a transmitting set encased in a polythene wrapper buried under the kitchen floor.

A signal plan lists instructions on times for listening or transmitting, and gives the necessary call signs and frequencies.

The 'one time' pads would have enabled them to transform figures or letters sent from Moscow to another set of figures or letters. There are several systems for this, but in all cases the resultant sets known as Groups are compared with a pre-arranged group in the Code Book to produce a word or series of words. *Without the book, nothing received over the air by Gordon Lonsdale or the Krogers could mean a thing.* Certain emergency signals would be familiar without the need for decoding, but nobody could know off by heart all the complexities of the book. As a general rule a series of groups containing about six numbers to one group are transmitted. This is where the 'one time' pads come in: the group of figures is subtracted from a known starting group in the pad, and the resultant group of figures presents what to look for in the Code Book.

With the discovery of the signal plans, the British Radio Detection Finding stations were able to pinpoint a transmitting station near Moscow as the source of the messages received in Ruislip. A communications specialist made a grand entry to the witness box during the trial and very theatrically described how it was all done.

Russia went on transmitting on these known frequencies, in accordance with the signal plan timetable, until 18th January. It would have been a great achievement for the British authorities to have been able to interpret those messages.

But there was no Code Book.

The Krogers didn't have it. Gordon Lonsdale didn't have it among his effects. Certainly neither Bunty nor I had it.

I have a pretty good idea where it went—or, rather, who went with it.

In such operations a key book of this kind is held by the person in command of the group, or cell. He alone is responsible for final decoding of messages, imparting to the others only such information as concerns them personally, under the 'need to know' formula.

I've never had any doubt who the leader of our particular lot was. It may have taken a day or two before he appreciated to the full just what had happened to us and the whole operation. It would certainly have been difficult, with communications abruptly cut off like that, for him to get word direct to Moscow to stop their transmissions. But at any rate he knew that there was little chance of those transmissions being correctly translated at this end, so long as he held the Code Book. Maybe he got it into Tony's hands—in Ireland, or maybe much further away. Maybe they both ran for it when the news broke.

I wonder where Roman is now?

Chapter Eleven

'D' Notice in Reverse

We now learned just how long we had been under observation. For the larger part of a year they had had tabs on Gordon Lonsdale and myself, and eventually got a line on the Krogers. Yet for months they didn't pounce—months during which, according to prosecution evidence in Court, secret information of great value was being transmitted to the enemy.

They can't have it both ways. Either the material I passed on was trivial, or it was important. If it was trivial, then the melodrama of the trial and the resultant savage sentences were unjustified. If it was important, why was the flow to Moscow allowed to continue so long?

The detached observer may give the authorities the benefit of the doubt and say they wanted to be scrupulously fair. They wanted to be absolutely sure before they rounded up the spies and made a clean kill.

But it can't be argued that they delayed because they wanted the whole gang in the net. They thought they *knew* the whole gang. Many months before the arrests, Gordon had led them to the Krogers and all the official statements show that they thought this completed the pattern.

It is the fundamental job of the police, secret or otherwise, to *prevent* crime. One move on their part and they could have put a stop to this crime: even if they hadn't been able to make a conviction stick early on, they could certainly have frightened us off and brought the operation to a standstill. Which was top priority: protection of national secrets, or prestige for the Security boys? Just as traffic cops are more interested in making arrests than in preventing accidents, so the Secret Police were more interested in obtaining a watertight conviction than in protecting their country.

The subsequent judicial process turned out to be not so much a trial as a propaganda exercise. This is admitted even in the attacks written immediately after the verdict by imaginative folk cashing in quick.

In 1960 the Western world had been set in a flurry by the shooting down of an American U2 spy plane over Russia and the taking alive of its pilot. After strenuous denials that such planes existed, the whole episode made for a lot of red faces among people whose beliefs and activities were far from Red. President Eisenhower had planned a Summit meeting with Khrushchev, de Gaulle and Macmillan for May 1960 in Paris, supposedly in search of world peace, having said in a speech some months earlier: 'Can we not join in a five-year or a fifty-year plan against mistrust and misgivings and fixations on the wrongs of the past?' The capture of U2 and pilot wrecked the Paris Summit and left the Eastern bloc laughing sourly about people who pontificated about 'mistrust' while continuing to behave in such a fashion.

Recriminations flew right, left and centre. There had to be a comeback.

The opportunity presented itself on 7th February 1961 when at Bow Street Magistrates' Court five of us were charged

> that they, in the Metropolitan Police District and elsewhere, between June 1960 and January 1961, unlawfully did conspire together and with other persons unknown to commit breaches of Section 1 of the Official Secrets Act, 1911.

Legal history was made by the appearance of the Attorney-General himself at the Magistrates' Court committal proceedings. Normally he would not have appeared until the case had been sent for trial at the Old Bailey, leaving the donkey-work in the lower court for his junior to do. But here was Sir Reginald Manningham-Buller—known far and wide as 'Bullying Manners'—well primed, and backed up by Mervyn Griffith-Jones, then Senior Treasury Counsel.

It has since been made clear that the Americans leaned hard on the British Government to exploit the trial as a propaganda answer to Russian jeers regarding their own activities; and the British fell into line. The big guns were brought up and started banging away right from the start.

While we were in custody, Bunty and I were allowed to write to each other. The letters were doubtless scrutinised a dozen times for hidden revelations about the spy ring, but we kept them purely personal, and said pretty well what we felt. Bunty's impression of 'Bullying Manners' was candid enough:

Strange when you see these people, they are nothing like one imagines, for instance I thought he would have been quite a gentleman. In fact he was rather more like some people behind stalls in Petticoat Lane.

In their book *Spy Ring*, John Bulloch and Henry Miller (Secker & Warburg, 1961) describe the performance as follows:

> The contrived theatricality of the hearing was part of the policy of maximum publicity. The Attorney General, not renowned for the lucidity of his speeches, had obviously prepared his brief with the most punctilious care and had been given the most expert advice. Certainly his opening statement was a masterly piece of work which would have been well received on any stage. In the setting of a court room it was an outstanding display of virtuosity.

The Government's Chief Censor at this time was the late Admiral Thompson. He was responsible for the issue of 'D' Notices, in peacetime a method of informing the Press that voluntary self-censorship should be exercised on news about hush-hush research and development projects, new equipment on the Secret List, or other topical matters which might be of use to an enemy. There is theoretically no compulsion to observe a 'D' Notice, but any newspaper failing to do so might find itself in bad odour and would probably be denied official Press facilities in future. In extreme cases the Editor could be prosecuted under the Official Secrets Act, so whilst the Government has no power to enforce its request it can take retaliatory measures if the request is not observed.

The Admiral put out a 'D' Notice just prior to the Magistrates' Court hearing, warning the Press that no attempt should be made to identify officers of MI5 and others who would not be referred to by name in Court. As this is normal Press practice, a special reminder was quite superfluous. The real function of the notice was to impress on the news media the importance the Government placed on the forthcoming trial, and it dropped one hefty hint regarding its real intentions:

> The Security Authorities are anxious to hold as little evidence as possible in camera as it is considered the public should be as

fully informed as national security permits regarding the facts of the case.

Governments aren't usually all that anxious to keep the public fully informed about anything whatsoever. It was all part of the same colourfully staged production which included such an early appearance of the Attorney-General. The invitation to keep the public informed was in fact a 'D' Notice in reverse—a clear indication that this was to be a propaganda trial. 'Foreign papers please copy,' as they used to say. The foreign correspondents certainly did copy, and passed the news lavishly around.

Even Bow Street No 1 Court was specially adapted for the benefit of the Press. Newspapers prepared to disseminate what the Government wished to be disseminated were in fact given priority over the public, who are supposed to be free to watch what goes on in their name. A new floor with raised benches was constructed in the public gallery for the use of reporters, and those few members of the public who did manage to gain admission were banished to a single narrow bench normally reserved for witnesses.

During his histrionic monologue, the Attorney-General declared a cold war on behalf of Great Britain and the United States against the Soviet Union. Knowing that his speech would be duly reported to Mr Khrushchev, he boomed a telling reply to the 'Spies over Russia' indictment which had shattered the Paris Summit. He didn't mince words by saying, as is usual during the preliminaries of such cases, that we were working for 'a foreign power' or even for an East European country. No, he waded right in and declared the information was being collected for Russia.

Accuracy played little part in the tirade. As one example from many, at one stage he referred to 'Most Secret' documents, when anyone conversant with security grading of documents knows there is no such classification: Secret or Top Secret, by all means, and at times I have even seen 'Not for Foreign Eyes' stamped on a document; but never Most Secret. No doubt it sounded more dramatic. In actual fact nothing was disclosed in evidence rating any classification higher than Secret. Bunty asked me what Most Secret was, and I had to confess my ignorance. Since our release she has told me that she never saw a Top Secret document in her life, which I believe.

In the face of such a barrage we ought, by all the boasted standards of British justice, have been allowed to mount an adequate defence. When we tried to do so, we speedily learned just what kind of a circus this was going to be.

On our arrest, all our assets had been impounded by Special Branch. In my case this involved all my cash, including £650 which the local police didn't find while searching my cottage and which I asked Detective Inspector Smith to recover for me from the garden shed, and £500 in Premium Bonds. My bank balance was frozen. Bunty's investments and Savings Certificates were also seized. Gordon's known assets suffered likewise, and I assume the same procedure applied to the Krogers.

I asked several solicitors if they would act for me. Each agreed to do so providing he could be 'placed in funds'. When I explained that all my own funds had been frozen, they suggested that I apply for Legal Aid and then get in touch with them again. I applied for Legal Aid. So did Bunty.

We both got the astonishing reply that it was considered we had sufficient assets to pay for our own defence. This from a Court which knew full well that the prosecution wouldn't allow us to touch one penny of those assets!

On the last afternoon of the committal proceedings Gordon asked formally on behalf of all of us for the return of the money seized by the police, so that we might draw on it to help pay for our defence. Mr Griffith-Jones objected on the grounds that 'This is Russian money'.

Not merely was most of my money not Russian, but in Bunty's case *the prosecution knew it was not Russian money*.

Bunty was dazed when giving evidence—who wouldn't be, with all the wigs and gowns fluttering and the world's Press greedy to make a meal of her?—and couldn't really believe that the irrefutable evidence of the purchase dates of her shares and savings certificates, going back for years and bought steadily, week by week, out of her salary, would be ignored. Her father and grandfather had both left her money, and this, too, had been tidily invested. There could have been no doubt in the minds of the prosecution about this: dates and figures were there to be seen. But they had been given their orders, and adherence to facts played little part in those orders.

One of Bunty's letters, after three days of revelations which were all utterly new to her, shows that, dumbfounded as she was by what I'd got her into she was equally dumbfounded by the workings of a legal system which she had been patriotically brought up to respect.

I'm sure anyone watching me in court would have said my eyes were standing out like organ stops. When they produced talcum powder tins with spare compartments, torches and whatnot it was more like a stage act but far above me. I wanted to keep asking what is it for? If all this is true my word we are in this with some of the worst people. On the other hand the share certificates they have taken of mine, quite a few are dated before the war, I was really mad about that and if they can stand up and say things about me like that one must doubt the truth of it all.

Then a Sunday newspaper came to Bunty's aid and provided money for her defence, and I know that Gordon raised some money from the now defunct *Sunday Dispatch*. For myself, on a major charge and with Legal Aid withheld, I was left at the end of the committal proceedings still without representation.

In the nick of time the Sunday newspaper which had bought Bunty's story agreed to buy mine also, and the fee was just enough to pay for my defence. Several times during the trial at the Old Bailey it occurred to me that the figure of Justice on the dome should have been surmounted by the flags of Fleet Street, who had provided three of the five of us with our only shield against the massive resources of the State.

How the Krogers fared, I don't know; but I imagined they paid for their defence from the proceeds of selling the Ruislip bungalow.

There was a blatant political motive in the withholding of Legal Aid. Plenty of people in far better circumstances than any of us—certainly receiving larger salaries than either Bunty or myself—have obtained Legal Aid for less serious offences. In 1965 there was a Chief Constable who, having been found guilty of a large number of charges of unlawfully using CID money, was reported to have cost the Borough Council (and therefore the ordinary ratepayer) £40,000 during the course of his long trial—his entire defence having been set up on Legal Aid. And then there was the story of Dr Emil Savundra, head of the ill-fated Fire, Auto and Marine Insurance Company, who, in spite of the rich life he had been so blithely living, and in spite of assets abroad and others in this country in his wife's name, also had the defence of himself and his managing director paid for by the public.

The position regarding entitlement to Legal Aid was straightened out a bit in 1968, and as the law stands now it is doubtful if either of those two cases quoted would have got full measure of free assistance. But as it stood in 1961, anyone seeking Legal Aid had to satisfy the Court that the charge was grave enough to warrant representation and that he hadn't enough money to meet likely fees. As we all, with the exception of Gordon Lonsdale, spent longer in prison than many sentenced to imprisonment for life, the charge was surely grave enough to warrant representation.

Most significant of all—in the September after we had been sentenced and deposited in prison, it was tacitly admitted that the money was rightfully ours, as after deduction of £1000 each from Bunty and myself 'towards costs', it was all returned to us. This did not, of course, get the kind of publicity that denunciations of 'Russian money' had had; in fact, it got none at all.

It was not until several years later that I learned how the scales of justice had been tipped even more weightily.

The defence knows nothing about the juror's personal life or politics: he or she is just an unidentifiable person called into the Court from the panel, and the defence has no idea of the background of such a person.

The *Daily Telegraph* of 3rd August 1966 carried an interesting report of how Viscount Dilhorne had told in a television interview of his having once asked a juror to stand down because he was an active member of the Communist Party. Asked by the interviewer about the problems of a Communist juror in spy or secrets cases, Lord Dilhorne said:

> I was very worried when I conducted those cases, that one might get a Communist on the jury because one disagreement in any of those cases, one juror disagreeing even though the case was very clear, would have meant a new trial, possibly followed again by disagreement, and abandonment of the prosecution.

When he spoke of the case being clear, Lord Dilhorne clearly meant that it was clear to him and must therefore be accepted by everybody else; and when he spoke of 'disagreement' he was clearly disapproving of anyone who disagreed with his own interpretation of the case. He went on to reveal:

> I did take steps in one of those cases to find out whether there were any well-known Communists on the jury panel and in fact I had to ask for one juror to stand down for the very reason that he was an active member of the Communist party.

The only spy or secrets trial in which Lord Dilhorne 'conducted' a case involving a Not Guilty plea and therefore involving a jury was the one in which he prosecuted us. Lord Dilhorne had at that time been, of course, Sir Reginald Manningham-Buller.

The defence knew nothing of this. The defence did not have the same facilities as the prosecution. If it was permissible for our accuser to remove from the jury any voice which might be raised against him for ideological reasons, ought not defending counsel have been granted access to enough personal information on jurors to weed out any Land-of-Hope-and-Glory types, ex-Naval people and others whose convictions or prejudices made their verdict a foregone conclusion?

How many of the public were aware that the jury panel had been investigated by the Secret Police to find out their political convictions?

How many were aware that three of the accused could afford a defence only by courtesy of Sunday newspapers?

How many were aware that we could not afford to call a single witness in our defence—could not afford the money or the time? There were several wild statements by the Crown and its agents which could easily have been refuted: easily, if we could have paid for the fares of defence witnesses, travelling to and from the West Country and elsewhere, for their loss of earnings and for the time they would have to stay in London during the hearing.

I'm not moaning about myself here. I went into the thing with my eyes open. But I am convinced that if we had had the facilities for calling truthful witnesses then Bunty, at any rate, would have stood a very good chance of an outright acquittal. Certainly she wouldn't have been savaged the way she was.

There's little doubt that Lord Parker, the Lord Chief Justice, was aware as he presided at the trial of some of these circumstances, but nothing was done to set them right. Indeed, on 12th April 1965, almost four years after he had imposed sentence, Lord Parker sanctimoniously stated in the House of Lords:

> It so happens that this June we in this country and in the United States are celebrating the 750th anniversary of Magna Carta. Your attention has been drawn to Chapter 40, which provides that to no one will we deny or delay right or justice. In the past there have been many attempts to prevent that principle, but all these we have resisted. Is it really to be said that in this 750th year we are to sweep all that aside? I am inclined to think your Lordships will give an emphatic "No!"'

An emphatic 'No'. Unless, of course, the Government wants to launch a propaganda salvo against a foreign Government.

British law is wonderful—if you can afford it. British justice...well, I'm not qualified to give an opinion: I've never encountered it so far.

The testimony I gave at the Old Bailey was pretty meaningless. I didn't dare to tell the true story of the Portland Spy Ring in the witness-box: it had to be tailored down to the best advantage. Swearing an oath to tell the whole truth, after hearing the majority of the witnesses against us perjure themselves up to the hilt, made the whole thing so grotesque that there didn't seem much point in trying to be either truthful or coherent. Four out of the five of us were sent to prison for crimes which we had committed: I'm not arguing that point. The length of our sentences, however, bore no relation to the gravity of our offence. We were sent to prison as a sacrifice to atone for the inefficiencies of the US and British Governments and their Security services.

Another fragment of a letter which I had from Bunty while we were still awaiting the outcome:

> If this goes on much longer when I do get out of here I think I will build a cell just like the one I'm in now, in a field miles away from anyone and only take in the milk and food by the window. One alteration I would make is a Dunlopillo bed. How my bones ache! but really I expect it is good for me.

In that same letter she went on to make plans for our maybe taking a little shop in another part of the country when we got out. She really did not understand that they were hell-bent on destroying her along with the rest of us, and that years of imprisonment lay ahead.

Chapter Twelve

Longer Than Life

The sentence meted out to Klaus Fuchs for putting Russia in possession of atomic secrets long before their own scientists could have worked them out was 14 years. Bunty and I were given 15 years each. The Krogers got 20 years, Gordon 25 years.

In passing sentence, the Lord Chief Justice said to Bunty: 'I think you acted for greed.'

What I did was done with my eyes open, and I'm not complaining unduly about the consequences. But as long as I live I shall never forgive that grotesque accusation, nor the savagery of the sentences handed out to the two women. They both served longer than the average 'life sentence', as, for that matter, did Peter Kroger and myself. It's well known among prisoners that anyone with a fixed long-term sentence is likely to be inside longer than one sentenced to imprisonment for life. Several convicted murderers who came in with a life sentence after our own arrival were released ahead of us.

Immediately after hearing the verdict I was utterly numb. When this wore off, there was the pain of knowing what I had done to Bunty. To this day I marvel at the fact that she has never reproached me. Not many women similarly placed would be so staunch.

After conviction and sentence we expected to be treated in exactly the same manner as other long-term prisoners. In fact we were treated as a class on our own, as this narrative will show.

The morning after Gordon Lonsdale, Peter Kroger and myself arrived at Wormwood Scrubs, we were interviewed by the civilian Tutor Organiser, who explained that we could enrol for various educational courses taking place after working hours. We all decided to take advantage of this, and enrolled for a number of courses. I don't remember what the other two put down, but I was accepted for an English class one evening a week and for the Spanish course, also one evening a week.

The cell doors were opened after tea at about a quarter to six and the men were escorted to the classrooms. But our doors weren't unlocked. We stayed where we were. On making enquiries the next day we were informed that we would not be allowed to participate in these extra-mural activities. No reason was given for this: they don't give reasons in prison.

This was just the start of the discrimination which was to continue throughout the whole period of my sentence. A couple of years later, when I was in Winchester prison, a very dedicated part-time Tutor Organiser came to my cell and asked if I would like to enrol for evening classes, but this time I refused point-blank. I wasn't going to give them another opportunity of telling me, after enrolment, that I couldn't attend the classes after all. During all those years I partook in no activity other than when compelled to do so. I shunned even the couple of hours 'Association' allowed in the evening after an initial period, when one could play chess, draughts or bridge, or watch TV: I stuck to my resolve to stay put in my cell.

Medical attention was on the same level. Asked by a prison doctor if I had any ailments, I said: 'Yes, I've got osteo-arthritis in both hips.' Without examining me he said this was quite untrue: I had no such thing. In fact it got worse under prison conditions, and nowadays is so bad in one hip that I need a stick most of the time. But the prison doctor's job is not to cure: it's simply to keep the inmates in 'a reasonable state of health', as they put it—in other words, to make sure they don't actually drop dead before they're tossed out into the outside world.

In common with other engaged prisoners, Bunty and I were allowed to write to each other. In the early days we received one free letter every two weeks and were allowed to purchase a letter from our 'wages' in the intervening week—if we could also afford the postage. As Bunty had so many relatives scattered all over the country, she had to space things out and so write to me every other week and to one of the family in the intervening weeks.

Letters to prisoners are of the greatest importance to their morale. Cut off as they are from the outside world, they long for some communication and long to know, as well, that their own messages have reached their destination. When an expected letter fails to arrive, frustration sets in, made worse by the inability to find out anything about it for oneself.

Strict censorship is exercised over outgoing letters. If you tell some uncomfortable truth about conditions inside, you are at once hauled up and admonished for saying things you shouldn't have said.

You're made to rewrite your letters, sometimes two or three times over, like downtrodden schoolkids.

Bunty and I were allowed a little more freedom, since our letters went only between prison and prison and not into the outside world. Some of Bunty's letters were the most outrageous black comedy: she was often depressed, often appalled by the hypocrisy and distortions around her—but she never cracked. We've saved all those letters, and one day they may see the light of day to show what a vicious farce the supposedly curative prison system of Britain in the 20th Century really is.

The freedom I've spoken of was only minor. Even these purely internal letters didn't always get through unbowdlerised. Worst of all, they rarely got through in reasonable time.

Normally the other prisoners' letters were not held up unduly, except by the usual GPO delays, and after being read by the uniformed censor were distributed, usually at dinner-time. Letters between Bunty and myself took far longer than any others. I have in my possession letters which took up to 23 days to get from Holloway to Winchester and vice versa. The average was, at best, about 10 to 12 days. Besides going via the ordinary censor, my letters were again censored by one of the civilian clerks: it's hard to imagine why, unless they thought two heads were better than one when it came to spotting sinister concealed messages. The same thing obviously happened at Holloway when Bunty wrote to me. Yet even this additional hurdle can hardly account for such a protracted hold-up. Maybe there was a third sleuth in the Home Office, checking we weren't planning an escape in code, or hoping to find some inadvertent remark which would put the Security Service on to something they had so far missed.

These repeated delays in getting letters from one another caused us both considerable mental distress. To anyone who has never been in such a situation, it may all seem trivial; but to the prisoner, and especially to a prisoner cut off from a loved one, it is overpoweringly real—and agonising.

Appeals to Governors were listened to sympathetically and always received the answer that the complaint 'would be looked into'; but they got us nowhere. Within the walls of his prison the Governor is king of the castle, but from outside the walls he has to take his instructions the same as anyone else—in this case from the Home Office.

Right up to the time of our release this deliberate harassment continued. In these more enlightened times prisoners are allowed one free letter a week and may purchase from their earnings up to two second-class or first-class letters as well. I don't know what changes in postal rates may have taken place by the time this book is in print, but when Bunty was in Styal prison the slower post cost 4d, the first class post 5d. Bunty decided to write to me by first-class mail so that I would hear from her more quickly, and the full fee was duly taken from her. In some cases these letters reached me unstamped, with a clear '5d' marking where the stamp ought to have been: the date heading of her letters showed they had been written several days previously. They had probably been enclosed in the OHMS official post, but this hadn't stopped the deduction of the full 5d from Bunty's meagre wages. Again, this may seem a small matter to an outsider. To a prisoner, 5d is a lot of money. A few such disappointments and irritations can come about through administrative blunders, but for them to go on year after year is more than accidental. We were the victims of a quite deliberate, sadistic campaign. The authorities know how obsessive such petty injustices can become in the constricted, unnatural world of prison. It had been decreed that we should suffer, and suffer we did.

Bunty got so frustrated by not being treated in the same fashion as other prisoners in the matter of mail that at one stage she wrote to tell me she wouldn't be humbugged any longer and that this would be the last letter she'd write to anyone. I told her that the only people who would profit from this would be the prison authorities, as it would mean fewer letters for them to censor, and the only people who'd be hurt would be those who loved her. However, she was adamant. It wasn't until we were allowed to meet some time later that I persuaded her to resume writing to her relatives and me.

Those meetings were another source of bitter feelings. We were sentenced in March 1961, and it was not until 15th October 1964 that we were permitted to see each other again. We both made representations through every channel available to us, starting with the Governors of our respective prisons, to the Visiting Magistrates who pay periodical visits, to an Assistant Director of Prisons whom I saw, and to the Home Secretary. All appeals fell on deaf ears. The Assistant Director casually passed off my plea by advising me to send a petition to the Home Secretary. Since the Home Secretary himself is unlikely to read through every appeal he receives, he would have passed it on to his relevant member of staff, who in this case would have been the bod I'd already spoken to and who already knew the answer was No.

We had been running around in circles getting nowhere until Bunty decided to write to the MP for her constituency, at that time Mr Guy Barnett. He took a humanitarian interest in the matter and was able to go right away to a much higher level. As a result the Home Secretary, then Mr Henry Brooke, authorised our seeing each other once every three months, and Mr Barnett informed Bunty accordingly.

Nevertheless it took the reluctant prison authorities ten weeks to arrange this meeting. It lasted thirty minutes and took place in the Governor's office at Holloway in the presence of one female and two male warders, who drank in every word we uttered. Bunty had to sit on one side of a desk and I on the other, in case we held hands.

We were, however, allowed to embrace when we met and when we parted. This at any rate was an improvement on our last encounter. After we had been sentenced at the Old Bailey I was allowed by a kindly Principal Officer to have a brief talk with Bunty before she was taken off to Holloway. When time was up I asked the warder if I could kiss her goodbye. Knowing full well that she was on her way to serve a fifteen-year sentence, the miserable, power-swollen bastard refused.

Anyway, now that the Home Secretary himself had authorised three-monthly visits we naïvely thought our visiting troubles would be settled. This was not to be. We had to fight every inch of the way, every time, for his orders to be implemented. Home Secretaries come and go but their permanent staff go on for ever, and resent the accepted order of things being tampered with.

Visits from friends didn't work out much more happily. The rule is that a prisoner may receive up to three visitors at the same time for thirty minutes once a month, or in some cases for only twenty minutes. He obtains a Visiting Order application, fills in the names of his friends, and an authorisation is sent out to them which they present at the gate, after which they are conducted to the visiting room.

An old friend of Bunty's who was also an acquaintance of mine wrote to say he was interested in Bunty's case and wanted to help her. Could he come and see me? I got a Visiting Order for him, but it took more than four weeks to reach him. Each prison has its own special visiting room, but when he arrived, instead of being conducted there, he was taken to a private room and a warder sat with us and openly took notes of the entire conversation. My visitor was a perfectly law-abiding and respectable citizen, who knew nothing about prison procedure before he came in; but he certainly knew plenty about certain aspects of it before he left, and was amazed.

I made a mental vow never again to put anyone in such a distasteful situation. As my visitors couldn't be treated in the same way as other visitors, and as I couldn't be treated in the same way as other prisoners, I wouldn't let such a thing happen again. Apart from Bunty I would see no-one.

The only exception I ever made to this rule was for a member of the Panel of Prison Visitors, who wouldn't be subjected to this humiliating treatment, to come and see me in Durham and Maidstone.

This Panel is a fine body of people. They voluntarily visit prisoners in their cells, usually about one evening a week. They have no connection with the prison staff and don't represent authority in any way. They are free citizens who care enough for their fellow creatures to leave their fireside and TV or anything else they may be doing and come into a dismal prison cell to chat to (or be talked *at* by) prisoners. I can't speak too highly of this devoted band who bring in a whiff of fresh air and help to break the grey monotony of prison existence. Invariably the talk gets round to the prisoner's grievances, real or imaginary, but they stick it like Trojans.

I had a Prison Visitor at Winchester whom I'm now glad to call a friend. He gave me a lot of encouragement when I was up against it, and when I was vindictively hustled off to Durham in circumstances which I'll describe later he wrote to ask if he and his wife could visit me. Time, distance, and personal inconvenience meant nothing to them. These two good people were the only exception I made to my vow not to receive visitors.

During my early few months at Wormwood Scrubs, before I'd reached this decision, I was visited every Sunday evening by a charming Canadian businessman who lived well out in Surrey but who, come hell or high water, left his family and turned up each week. He has since returned to Canada. And whilst I was in Maidstone a delightful old naval man, over seventy years old, called on Friday evenings. The theme of our conversation was invariably 'The ships I've been in and the bastards I served under'. Time always passed too quickly with him. I called him Woodbine Willie, as he never failed to produce a cigarette during our little natter. He had been coming regularly to that 'nick' for more than twenty-six years. More power to his elbow—and the others like him.

In general, within the prison itself, I was treated the same way as the others by the warders. I did run into the odd one who took it on himself to make things hard for me—but that happens to everyone inside, sooner or later. The bad screws were no worse to me than they were to the remainder.

A screw's word is of course always accepted by prison Governors in preference to a prisoner's, so if you do happen to run foul of one you're in trouble. There's no redress. Several times I've known of stuff being planted in a man's cell and then of the man being brought in front of the Governor, of men being wrongfully accused of swearing at a screw or of insolence. It was an offence to look out of the cell window: the window being high in the wall, it's necessary to climb up on a chair-back to see out, and I've known of men being reported for this who were actually lying on their bed at the time alleged. If a prisoner, goaded beyond endurance, lays a hand on a screw he doesn't just get the official punishment: he gets a private beating-up by the heavy mob in the punishment cells as well. Any injuries received are always attributed to the force needed to restrain him.

On the other hand, I personally received many acts of kindness which deserve to be placed on record. Decent treatment, a kind word, even a 'good morning' was much appreciated. Several times I've had a cigarette from a screw. One Christmas morning a decent bloke came into my cell, dug his hand into his back pocket, and brought out a flask of rum. 'Here you are, Harry—an ex-naval type like you, you can see it all off.' This man risked a stiff reprimand and possibly losing his job, the quarters that went with it, his eventual pension, if this act of kindness were found out. As I spent nine Christmas mornings in various prisons it would be impossible now for anyone to pinpoint my benefactor, so I can mention this without fear of the consequences.

Another different act of kindness was performed when I was in the Special Security Wing at Durham. I developed a corn on the ball of my foot and, having nothing to trim it with, was in considerable pain. A hospital screw happened to be in the wing one day and asked if I'd got something wrong with my foot. When I'd told him what was wrong, he took me into the office and, after I'd removed my shoe and sock, trimmed the corn there and then with a surgical knife he carried in a compact. It didn't end at that: about every two weeks during my stay in the Special Security Wing he made a special trip to do that corn. Another example of what may seem small and inconsequential to an outsider, but meant a hell of a lot to the person concerned.

At times one met a 'bent' screw—that is, one who would bring in tobacco, spirits or even food at inflated prices. He would also pass letters out at a price: for some reason not clear to me, these letters are called 'stiffs' by the inmates. These crooked screws are few and far between, and during my whole time inside I met less than two handfuls of fingers. The straight ones are constantly on the lookout for their bent colleagues and have no qualms whatsoever about reporting them if they get even a sniff of illicit dealings with prisoners.

I hadn't been in Winchester a fortnight when, during the dinner hour, my cell door was unlocked and one of them said: 'What about a hacksaw blade?' Though I wasn't the least little bit interested in sawing through the bars of my window (after all, you weren't *supposed* to stand on a chair), I was curious, and enquired: 'How much?' The answer was: 'Fifty quid.' I gave a firm 'No', he went out, and that was the end of that. I didn't consider it my business —or in the interests of my health—to report this.

Up to the time when Charles Wilson, one of the Great Train Robbers, escaped from Winson Green it would have been comparatively easy for me to have got away. I had several offers of assistance from men due for release: one even got himself sent back to prison for a short spell to inform me that he could fix me a motor cruiser on the Hamble River to get me over to the Continent at a cost of £500. I was not prepared to entertain any idea of escape: whatever my own fate might be, the consequences to Bunty were bound to be appalling. Just how appalling they could be in such circumstances, we were not to discover until October 1966.

The plan itself was quite simple. At that time prison security wasn't too tight, and anyone with enough money to pay for an escape and with friends to organise it could, if he really tried, get away. All locks on cell doors were being changed for a new pattern, and although precautions were taken to ensure that prisoners assisting in the work involved should not get a chance of seeing the new key, not only did they see it but took an impression for future reference. A duplicate key of the outer doors of the block was already floating about the prison, and although these outer doors were double-locked at night it was a simple matter for a couple of chaps to get over the wall, enter the cell block, overpower the night watchman if necessary, unlock me—or anyone else—and then off over the wall to a waiting car, the Hamble, and freedom. The solitary patrol on the inner perimeter of the prison wall could easily have been overpowered if he had been awake. In fact, apart from the feature of the cabin cruiser, a very similar method was used to get Charles Wilson out of Winson Green a couple of years later. At that time security was so slap-happy that the outer doors of the cell blocks didn't even have an inside bolt: anyone with a key could get in. After Wilson's escape, there was a hurried change. Bolts and padlocks were fitted on the inside the very same day. Unfortunately the reinforced night staff found themselves without keys for these new padlocks and so were unable to get out on the first night of the new régime—they were locked in, just the same as the prisoners.

Other escape overtures were made to me. Some were feasible and some quite ridiculous. It was difficult to put over to the would-be planners that I just wasn't interested in escaping. Even if I'd been desperate enough to have a go, there would always have been the danger of someone with a long time to serve getting wind of it and, hoping to be rewarded with extra remission, blowing the gaff. There is no honour among thieves; nor is there any honour among certain types of prisoner who curry favour by keeping eyes and ears open and reporting anything at all untoward. In most cases the screws—which means, in effect, the Governor—wouldn't know the feeling inside the nick if it weren't for these informers. They get short shrift from other prisoners if they're found out.

In all prisons there is a Principal Officer in charge of Security. At Maidstone he was known as Security Syd, and Syd was invariably one jump ahead of most potential breaches of discipline. One Sunday morning there was to be a sit-down strike at exercise as a protest, I think, about the lousy food. Syd got to know, and that morning there was no exercise period. Cannabis was being introduced into the nick: Syd got to know, and blocked further supplies. Porno books from Denmark were being freely passed around: Syd found them, not by skilful detection but via his informers.

I remained in the slum called Wormwood Scrubs for two months and then, without warning, a warder came into my cell and told me to roll up my bedding and come with him. I found myself in no time at all in a van, handcuffed to another warder. I didn't know where I was bound, but could see we were headed in a southerly direction. My escort eventually thawed out and said I was going to Winchester. Normally prisoners are notified not later than the preceding day if they are due for a transfer, but in accordance with my special treatment this didn't apply in my case. So I exchanged one slum for another, though it has to be admitted that there's more whitewash splashed about on the landings at Winchester than at the Scrubs.

It's a marvel there has never been a serious epidemic in 'C' Hall at Wormwood Scrubs. Hundreds of men are crowded in there, generally three to a cell, built more than a hundred years ago to house one occupant in each cell. Apart from the provision of a different type of bed and a lumpy (and often filthy) mattress stuffed with coconut fibre, plus a low power electric bulb, the interiors have not changed over the century. Although thousands of pounds have been spent to convert the old coal and coke heating systems to oil, the heat does not penetrate the cell walls: there is a cavity built into the walls for heat to rise from underground pipes, but over many a decade these cavities have become blocked with falling masonry, mortar and dead pigeons, so that in cold weather the cells are like refrigerators.

And the smell...! Try to imagine several hundreds of men who have been confined in their cells for periods of up to fourteen hours and so unable to get out to obey the call of nature—imagine them all emptying their chamber pots at seven o'clock in the morning. Three men in a cell means three chamber pots. The occupants have to sleep with this stench all around them. In recent years the recesses where the pots are emptied have had the walls tiled instead of being whitewashed, and in some cases an exhaust fan has been fitted into the window bars; but no exhaust fan yet invented can entirely take away this lingering smell.

And still they preach about prison being educational and reformative, fitting the wrongdoer to take his place in civilised society when at last he is released. Short of shitting on the carpet twice a day and leaving it there, I can't see how any ex-prisoner can dutifully practise outside what he has learnt inside.

It was hard to understand why I was being spirited away to Winchester, a 'local' prison, when I was already in a long-term central prison.

I should explain that a local prison, such as Winchester, is a receiving prison from Magistrates' Courts, Quarter Sessions and the Assize Court of the county in which it is situated. Long-term prisoners are moved after a short period to a central or 'long-term' prison, while those serving a short-term sentence usually remain in the local one. It has been the policy to segregate first offenders, or Star prisoners as they are called, from the regular customers—presumably so that they shouldn't be further contaminated. There were three Star central prisons: Wormwood Scrubs, Wakefield, and Maidstone. Discipline in local prisons is much more severe than that in the central prisons, maybe in the belief that a short sharp lesson will ensure that first offenders don't come back. My conclusion is that the decision to transfer us to this sort of place was another feature of the Government's policy to give us as rough a time as possible. Bunty and Mrs Kroger were shifted from Holloway and sent to Birmingham and Manchester respectively, and remained there until those prisons ceased to have women's wings, when they were shunted back to Holloway. Peter Kroger was sent to Manchester, Gordon Lonsdale to Birmingham.

Quite a few faces in these different settings became familiar. Regular customers such as petty thieves, gas meter bandits, debtors and maintenance men came, served their sentences, and reappeared with monotonous regularity. If any of them failed to show up after a reasonable time, one wondered what had become of them: it generally transpired that they had been picked up in another county and so were in another prison.

When it dawned on me that I was, down to the tiniest detail, being discriminated against by the authorities, I had to make up my mind whether or not to complain about this selected treatment. Did they want to know it was hurting? Did they want me to lash out in a fit of despair, so that they could dock any remission I was entitled to? After long and careful thought I decided against complaining, even though I was seething inside. Whatever I was in prison for, it wasn't to give these bureaucrats satisfaction. The only thing I continually pressed for was to see Bunty.

Having opted to take no part in any extra-cellular (if there is such a word) activities, I was locked in my cell from about 4.45 pm until 7 am next morning, and all day Saturday and Sunday. The problem was what to do with the time on my hands. I decided eventually to make a tapestry bedspread. I had the materials sent in, and after a couple of false starts got the hang of it and evolved a patchwork design of my own. There are more than 120,000 stitches in the finished article. How do I know this? Because, having little else to do, when I'd finished the job I counted them.

Having served the three years specified in regulations, I was permitted to send out for a transistor radio, which was a great boon. New horizons opened up. The radio was my best friend in prison. Now I could keep abreast of world affairs without being interrupted in the laborious construction of my bedspread. I must have been the best informed man in the prison—including the staff—on current affairs. I listened to little other than radio talks, not being much interested in pop music. As I was the only prisoner at Winchester who had served the required three years, mine was the only radio allowed, so I was in great favour during the afternoons when racing results were announced.

There was a time when possession of this radio could have landed me in trouble, if one of the warders had had his way. The man in the adjoining cell had obtained a hacksaw blade and was diligently sawing through the bars of his window when he got caught in the act. The particular screw who caught him stormed into my cell and accused me of aiding and abetting a prisoner attempting to escape by drowning the noise of his hacksaw activities with my radio. The Chief Officer was brought in, and accepted my view that what the man in the next cell does is his own affair and that it wasn't up to me either to assist or to hinder him. I was asked if I'd known what he was doing. I replied that I couldn't see through twelve inches of brick, but that even if I had known it was none of my business, and as a prisoner I was not there to do their job for them.

I was allowed to continue my solitary course in self-education in world affairs.

At no time did I ever come across any attempt by the prison authorities to reform anyone. Despite the unctuous utterances of those who earn a comfortable living from administering prisons, the emphasis is, rightly or wrongly, on punishing the criminal, notwithstanding that deprivation of liberty is in itself punishment enough. One screw always informed newcomers: 'You're here for punishment, and I'm here to carry it out—always remember that, and you'll get on all right.' Maybe the majority of the public and the majority of the legal profession believe this is sound policy. Fair enough; but at least let's drop the pretence of enlightened administration and the curative properties of a spell in jail. On hearing a man quietly humming to himself whilst sewing his mailbag, another screw bawled out: 'Stop singing, there. Prisoners have no right to be happy.'

The only reformative effort I ever saw was initiated not by the prison authorities but by a prisoner himself, who at Maidstone got permission to form a branch of Alcoholics Anonymous. A prison Welfare Officer interested himself in the movement and introduced outside speakers to the meetings, and generally paved the way for the provision of facilities which otherwise would probably not have been approved. I sometimes wonder if anyone reaped any ultimate benefits: I hope so...but it's easy enough to swear off drink when none is available, and the real proof of success would be when the members were discharged from prison and subjected to the usual temptations.

Most thieves have no desire to be reformed. They have a way of life like anyone else: thieving is their trade or profession, and their main intention is to make a better job of things next time and not get caught. Many have told me that they intend to stop when they hit the jackpot and can sit back to enjoy the proceeds. Very few, if any, realise this ambition. They come back to prison with bigger and better sentences each time.

Those who genuinely long to reform don't often have the strength of character to do so when they get out. One man I got to know quite well was serving five years for rape. He appeared deeply remorseful, and applied to go to the psychiatric prison at Grendon Hall in the hope of a cure. The Home Office medical people approved of this—which, incidentally, saved his marriage breaking up at that juncture—so away he went. A couple of years later I read that he had been sentenced to seven years' imprisonment for a similar offence, the judge describing him as a beast. This beast was a quite intelligent man who will, I fear, spend most of his life in prison through being unable to control his emotions. There is a sane, compassionate way of preventing it all happening again to innocent women, but English law—unlike that applying in Denmark—will not permit it.

Sexual offenders get a very rough passage in prison from other inmates, especially when the offence is committed against a child. I witnessed many acts of brutality, even under the very noses of the warders, many of whom turn their backs on such assaults. It's a horrible crime to overpower and rape women or commit indecent acts against children; but this has already been taken into consideration by the judge trying the case and is reflected in the sentence imposed. But many prisoners feel they have a divine right to add their own punishment to the judge's. It is perfectly in order to cosh an elderly postmistress in furtherance of a robbery, or to batter some ageing person for their money or valuables, or for a gang with pickaxes to attack ordinary working people legitimately carrying their employers' cash; but it is *not* all right to commit certain other offences.

A sex offender has great difficulty in keeping the knowledge of his offence secret. Even though he may have been transferred from a prison many miles away, there are always members of the staff who delight in passing on the man's pedigree to his fellow prisoners. Bad cases can, and often do, ask for protection, which means they work in their cells and exercise under close supervision. They are still not immune from assault. It frequently happens that when the man's meal is taken to his cell by a prisoner, hot tea will 'accidentally' be poured over him as his mug is being filled. Should his cell door be inadvertently left unlocked whilst he is out on exercise or for some other reason, more than likely when he returns he will find his bedding smeared with excreta and his drinking mug full of urine.

So the years went by at Winchester, one day much the same as the next except that once a week there was a bath. Officially there were twenty minutes allowed for this from the time of leaving the workshop to time of resuming work. A clean shirt, vest, shorts, socks, handkerchief and a huckaback towel were issued on emerging from the bath. These articles, plus a pair of trousers, a jacket, one pair of shoes, a bib and brace overall and a spare shirt to be used as a nightshirt, were all the kit issued in local prisons. The clean underwear, socks and handkerchief came from a communal kitty: if anything fitted, you were fortunate. A woollen pullover was issued in cold weather. I never had a hat on my head for more than nine years, irrespective of the weather.

While I plodded my way through this, Bunty had been sent into exile. Having proved a model prisoner, she was transferred to Styal in Cheshire, sometimes misleadingly referred to as an 'open prison'. It is no such thing; but at least the régime is a little easier, and the buildings are less primeval than those of Holloway.

The whole thing was, though, that Bunty hadn't wanted to go. It took her far out of visiting range for her 86-year-old mother who, because of increasing infirmity, couldn't possibly travel that far—especially when all that awaited her at the end of such a journey was the briefest of interviews. Bunty made repeated representations to be sent back to Holloway, in spite of its miseries, simply for her mother's sake. Pleas were put forward from outside to the Home Office on Mrs Gee's behalf. They made no impression whatsoever. The old lady spent the closing months of her life fretting over her inability to summon up sufficient strength to travel from Dorset to Cheshire. Yet Bunty and I know of a prisoner who was returned without fuss to Holloway merely on the grounds that she 'didn't like it' at Styal; and before long, as I shall tell, the authorities shifted Bunty herself back to Holloway at a few minutes' notice when it suited them.

The only time Bunty saw her mother again was when the old lady was on her deathbed. The Home Office relented sufficiently to allow her one hour at the bedside. But her mother was too far gone by then, and died without knowing that Bunty was there.

In time, Bunty became accustomed to life at Styal. She became librarian there, moved about fairly freely, trusted and untroublesome. Late in 1966 she was brought to Holloway for one of our meetings, and went back in a philosophical frame of mind. One of her letters from Styal sums things up well:

> You know this is the first time since I have been in the 'Nick' that I really have known peace of mind from outside, and if this continues I can do till 1971 standing on my head! The everyday affairs of this life simply pass over me like so much water. I often feel like a person outside looking in and there is so much that is funny about it—I mean funny Ha! Ha!...
>
> At least I think I am fortunate in being able to interest myself in *anything* I'm doing. You see I have no intention of looking on this as a punishment. I'm simply not willing to be punished, so I regard it simply as the means of passing the time quickly, also I am on my own most of the time which means much in these places, I do not have to listen to hard luck stories, one can become so weary hearing how well off and what big shots these people were outside, if one believed it they are doing us a favour in letting us mix with such people.

Bunty's calm, resigned mood didn't last long. It wasn't given the chance to do so.

One Saturday evening I was overjoyed to hear on my radio that the man serving the longest fixed prison sentence in English legal history had escaped. I'd never met him, knew precious little about him personally; but somehow the news was cheering, and I wished him well and hoped he wouldn't be recaptured.

He wasn't recaptured. Neither Bunty nor I could, in our worst nightmares, have foreseen what the repercussions would mean to us.

Chapter Thirteen

The Blake Penance

On the night of 26th October 1966 I turned in after the issue of cocoa at 8 pm. In the early hours of the morning I was woken up by the cell light being suddenly switched on. Two warders came in and told me to get ready, as I was on the move. Still blinking my way out of a sound sleep, I could hardly take this in; but whether I could take it in or not, it was true. Haste was the watchword: a quick wash and then to reception, where a mug of what passes in prison for tea was waiting. I suppose there must have been a breakfast, too, but I've no recollection of eating it.

I asked what on earth had happened, and where I was going. This, I was told, had to be a secret until I'd left the prison. The Governor then came on the scene and told me he was sorry I had to go. The decision to move me had been taken by the Home Office. He went so far as to shake hands with me and wish me well.

It didn't sound any too cheering.

Outside in the half-light of dawn I was put in a Hampshire Constabulary car and handcuffed to a warder. There was a second warder on my other side, and a sergeant and a constable in the front. At a nod from the Head of Hampshire CID, who had also turned out of bed to ensure that I got away in due order, the gates of the prison opened and we began the hair-raising journey to Durham. As soon as we left the prison they told me it was going to be Durham for me. I had no illusions then: it obviously meant the infamous Special Security Wing.

Never have I travelled so fast on land as we went that day. We headed first for Nottingham prison, and no car can ever have done the journey from Winchester to Nottingham in a shorter time. Instead of being taken to the reception block for a meal, as would have been the case with any other prisoner in transit who had to stop off there, I had my dinner in the punishment block. From there on it was non-stop to Durham.

In retrospect it's laughable what frightened fools the authorities were. No one was remotely interested in freeing either Bunty or myself. Yet as the car crossed the border between one county and another, each Chief Constable seemed to have the idea that the most dangerous criminal the country had ever produced was passing through his territory and that Russians lurked under every bush ready to pounce and free me. Often on that mad journey the two warders and two policemen in the car were supplemented by another two men in another car leading the convoy, plus a police car in the rear containing two more policemen, followed by a van containing a police dog and its handler. So it took at least nine men and a dog to get me to Durham—nine men and a dog at any given time, I mean, since cars dropped out and were replaced by others at the county boundaries. This takes no account of the motor-cycle police who appeared as from nowhere at road intersections and blocked off traffic so we could have right of way. Royalty never had clearer roads than I did.

Passing Scotch Corner on the A1 I noticed we were doing 93-mph, and commented to the driver that Barbara Castle, then Minister of Transport, would have twins if she could see us doing that speed. One of the escort rejoined that she'd have triplets if she had to sit in the back as we were doing.

Another bit of hindsight: at the very time such massive precautions were being taken to ensure that I didn't get loose and contaminate the countryside, a homicidal convict, Frank Mitchell, known as the Mad Axeman, was happily swanning off from Dartmoor working parties and going on carefree pub crawls entirely free of any supervision.

On arrival at Durham I realised my forebodings were justified. It was straight to the special Security Wing for me. After being thoroughly searched— what for, I don't know, as I'd been handcuffed to a warder all the way from Winchester except for my hurried midday meal—I was bunged into a specially reinforced cell with extra bars on the window, like the majority of cells in that section. Some of the bars were connected to an electrical circuit which would set off an immediate alarm in the control room if touched, and the door was wired in such a way that the control room could see on a tell-tale whether it was open or shut. I was given a meal in my cell on a chipped enamel plate, and a plastic mug of tea, and left to my own devices with nothing to do and nothing to read.

Later, as I found was the custom at that time, two warders came and demanded all my clothing except for my shirt but including my vest. I had to put it all in a cardboard box together with my shoes and socks. This box was then taken away to be locked in a cell along with the clothing of the other inmates of the wing. Being naked except for my shirt, I had nothing to do but get into bed. A yellow light was left burning in the cell all night. This was to be my lot for months to come. It was rather a waste of electricity, since the outside of the Special Security Wing was illuminated as though for Son-et-Lumière, and even without the cell light the brightness from outside would have been more than sufficient for anyone looking through the Judas Hole in the door to see what I was doing.

In the mornings the cell door was unlocked and the box containing my clothes was thrust inside, the door being locked again at once. Besides the usual lock there were four sets of bolts—security gone mad. The next time the door opened it was to allow me to empty my chamber pot, a process officially known as slopping out, and to fill my water jug for my morning toilet. Every inmate of the wing had to slop out individually: no two cell doors were open at any one time, and four warders supervised the operation. A razor was issued, and collected again after shaving. All the blades had to be accounted for. Then breakfast was brought, always cold, as it had had to be brought from the main prison. One ate it off a chipped enamel plate. All enamel plates in all prisons are chipped.

After breakfast the Humiliation Process was put into force. The prison uniform of grey trousers and jacket which I had worn in Winchester and in which I had travelled from there was taken away from me. On the floor lay a number of uniforms which would have brought a laugh if worn in the ring by a circus clown. I had the degrading experience of having to pick out from the floor a previously used and not cleaned Harlequin uniform which would more or less fit—less rather than more. This consisted of grey trousers with a broad, bright yellow stripe running from waist to ankle on each leg, back and front, and a jacket with a large yellow patch on the front. The prime object was to humiliate: nothing can make a human being look and feel more idiotic than to be forced to dress in such outrageous garb.

I was then told that I had to undergo 28 days of solitary confinement, but would be allowed the statutory 30 minutes exercise twice a day.

What had I done to merit such punishment?

Exercise took place under heavy guard in a high walled courtyard measuring 14 paces by 14 paces. Coils of barbed wire ran round the top, but the camouflage netting which completely covered the compound when it was used by the Great Train Robbers was for some reason not in place. Later the exercise varied between this compound and a slightly larger one with higher walls, with the usual barbed wire midway up the walls and a covered lookout box perched on top: I used to think of it as the Berlin Wall of Durham.

According to photographs I saw later, the larger of the two compounds has now been converted into a cage by the installation of high chain linked fencing on the inside, topped by barbed wire coils. There men are reduced to animal status. Maybe society has to have its pound of flesh from evildoers, but vengeance is being extracted in a terrible way when the only breath of fresh air which men are allowed is from within a cage. To anyone in his early thirties I would ask: think back on your life so far, your earliest memories, your childhood, school years and school holidays, your first job or perhaps a period in the armed forces; think of college or university, courting days, marriage and the raising of a young family, and all the events in between...and then think of men who during all that time will have seen the sky and breathed outside air for only two periods of 30 minutes a day (providing the weather is suitable) from within a cage. Most of the men serving these extremely long fixed sentences, with no remission for good conduct, are murderers, and I can imagine the relatives of their victims rubbing their hands in glee: they'd not be human if they didn't. But really isn't this retribution a bit too long-drawn-out?

During my solitary confinement I was given the inevitable prison task of sewing mailbags, which brought me an average wage of 5s.3d. a week. There were no restrictions about smoking, other than those caused by shortage of tobacco, and I used my money on this indulgence. Opportunities for any other kind of self-indulgence were non-existent. Up to six library books could be obtained each week, so I passed my time sewing and reading.

I resented this solitary confinement on the principle that by statutory rules a prison Governor can only award up to 14 days solitary for an offence against prison discipline which he thinks merits it. A longer term than that has to be dealt with by a board of Visiting Magistrates. Yet here I was doing 28 days without having committed any offence at all.

Representations were made on my behalf to Alice Bacon about this, and received the fatuous Ministerial reply that this period was not to be regarded as punishment but had been imposed on Home

Office instructions 'to see how he fitted into the régime at Durham'.

So it wasn't a punishment. That ought to have made me feel a lot better. Strangely enough, it didn't.

In the meantime there was no news of Bunty, but at first it didn't occur to me that anything could be seriously wrong. I wrote to Styal as usual, not knowing—and not being told by anyone—that she was no longer there. She, not knowing I was in Durham, continued to write to me at Winchester. When her letters at last caught up with me, they told a story even more outrageous than my own.

As I've recorded earlier, Bunty had settled into a philosophical routine at Styal, where she was trusted and allowed considerable freedom of movement. She wore her own clothes, and if at any time she had wanted to escape she could probably have sauntered out without her absence being noticed for quite some time.

In her librarian's job she often had to work after tea when the remainder of the prisoners were locked up. On that fateful evening when I had decided to turn in early, only to be so rudely awakened, Bunty was hard at it in the library until 8 pm. She then closed the place and, as was her custom, walked unescorted to her quarters. When she got there she found she had been locked out. There was no wardress inside to let her in, so she had to cruise around the prison looking for someone with a key. The Styal administration can hardly, in such circumstances, have regarded her as a serious escape risk.

She set off quite normally the next morning for the library, but wasn't destined to get there. Abruptly she was seized by the shoulder and hustled to reception. There she was bundled into a car with an escort and driven close to her quarters, where one of the escort got out, collected her belongings, and chucked them into the boot. Then it was hell for leather, with police escort front and rear, to Holloway. For her as for me, cars and motor-cyclists appeared at county boundaries, roads were cleared, and I imagine innumerable Chief Constables must have been sitting around twitching until we were safely out of their region.

It hadn't suited the powers that be to allow Bunty to stay in or be brought back to Holloway at any time so that her ageing mother could visit her. But it suited them now.

Bunty was put into a cell and was trying to settle in when it was decided than an ordinary prison cell with a lock on the door and bars at the window wasn't designed well enough to hold such a desperate creature. She was peremptorily ordered to go under escort to sleep in a cell in the Borstal wing. Bunty refused. After arguments and threats the Governor of Holloway was called to the scene and ordered that Bunty was to be forcibly removed to the Borstal wing. Four women screws hauled her away struggling to what she has described as the filthiest cell she ever had the misfortune to see. During the struggle strict orders were given by the Governor that she was 'not to be marked'.

A light was kept burning in the cell all night, a misery she was to experience for many months to come. The place being so filthy, she didn't remove her clothes or lie on the dirty mattress, but sat in a chair and dozed fitfully all night.

And all this within twenty-four hours of banging on the door in another prison after dark and asking to be let in!

Why had we been turned on so savagely?

My moment of jubilation over the radio announcement of that escape had been premature. The escaper was George Blake, sentenced to 42 years imprisonment as a spy.

The Blake affair had been a major embarrassment to the British Government in the first place. Supposedly one of our most reliable Secret Service agents, he had in fact been working for the Russians, one of the top double agents of all time. Now he had cheated them again, by breaking out and, most appalling of all, getting away scot-free.

Somebody had to suffer.

None of us had ever had any connection whatsoever with Blake. We operated in quite different fields. We knew nothing of him before he was imprisoned, and we did nothing to assist his escape. Nevertheless the Home Office chose us as the scapegoats. Attacked by critics from all sides, Mr Roy Jenkins and Miss Alice Bacon tightened up the statutory prison rules against five people who had no way of answering back, or even of uttering an appeal that would be listened to.

Helen Kroger received the 'treatment' in Holloway, just as Bunty was doing. Peter Kroger, like myself, was humiliated—in his case, in Parkhurst—by being made to wear the same kind of Tom Fool's uniform and was also given 28 days solitary confinement—presumably to see how he 'fitted into the régime'.

After five years and nine months as a model prisoner, Bunty's conditions were infinitely worse than they had been at the beginning.

Her letters from Holloway were quite different—pathetically so—from that cheerful one I had so recently had from her at Styal.

> I am worse off now than at any time during the past 5½ years. Am living (if one could call it that) on the wing where I always was. At 8 o'clock each night I have to be taken up to the Borstal wing to sleep, and I do mean sleep, for it is so cold one must get into bed quickly and even then it is too cold to read... My radio is taken from me. Visits are also stopped apart from a 30-min. closed visit, so have not sent out to anyone, it is much too far for so short a time.
>
> By and large I am just about at the end of my tether, will try to give it a month to see what happens, but I don't know, I just can't take much more of this, the thought of another 4½ years of it one would be far better off dead. When I think that only the last night at Styal I was fool enough to go knocking on the door asking to be let in!

Every night someone crept along the passage at intervals and peered in through the spy-hole, making just enough noise to wake her up.

In Durham it was ordained that the four first offenders there should be given a period of 'Association' after tea from about 6 pm. to about 7.45. This meant all four being locked in a cell with a cell table and draughts and chess provided. Later they were allowed to mix with the rest on the ground floor, where there were a ping-pong table, weight-lifting classes, and TV.

I wouldn't want, incidentally, to confirm the popular misconception that the taxpayer provides TV and other treats for pampered prisoners. All such amenities are paid for by the inmates, whether they participate or not, through money compulsorily deducted from their sparse earnings.

For myself, cocoa was issued at 7.45 pm and my clothes were taken away. Having been summarily deprived of my radio, there was nothing for it but to go to bed with a book.

Tea on Saturdays and Sundays, high days and holidays was at 4 pm, so cocoa was issued and I had to hand in my clothes at 6 pm. This also happened on Christmas night, when it was so cold that I couldn't take my hands out from under the blankets to turn the pages. I spent long hours wondering how Bunty was being treated on this day of peace and goodwill—and devising what I'd like to do, given the opportunity, to Roy and Alice, who at this season were probably gracing Party and charitable functions without so much as a passing thought for the woman they had decided to punish for another's escape.

Bunty made representations about her treatment through the official channels: the Governor, Visiting Magistrates, the Home Secretary himself. All to no avail. Lord Stonham, who succeeded Alice Bacon as Minister of State, Home Office, came to see her in her cell when she was later removed to the specially adapted Special Security Wing; but, probably out of loyalty to his predecessor and without regard to the merits of the case, stipulated that she was to remain there. Mr Evelyn King, then MP for her constituency, took up her case with the Home Secretary and stressed that a light was kept burning in her cell day and night and that privileges which she had earned had been withdrawn through no fault of her own. But the punishment remained. We called it the Blake Penance.

When Frank Mitchell, the Mad Axeman, finally tired of strolling around Dartmoor's pubs and was freed by some friends, there was no immediate clamp-down on other homicidal maniacs in custody. We had been singled out for special treatment from the start; the pattern was at any rate consistent.

A privilege granted in all English prisons is for prisoners to buy from their own money one daily and one Sunday newspaper, and a weekly or monthly periodical. This was one of the few privileges not withdrawn from inmates of the Special Security Wing. For reasons known only to the authorities, in some prisons the exchange of newspapers between prisoners is regarded as one of the seven deadly sins. At Winchester it was a rule that the previous day's paper had to be handed back before the current one was issued. At Durham, however, exchange of newspapers between prisoners was permitted.

One Sunday evening in 1966 the Governor, Major George Bride —called 'Old George' by the prisoners, though not to his face— came to my cell with the *Sunday Express* in his hand and asked: 'Have you seen this rubbish?'

'This rubbish' was the product of a *Sunday Express* reporter's fertile imagination, describing how Bunty and I had been stopped writing to each other on instructions from the Home Office. It was quite untrue. This was, in fact, just about the only dirty trick the Home Office hadn't played on us.

It was the Governor's weekend off. He explained that he had been watching TV at home when his daughter drew his attention to the article on how Bunty and I were being penalised. He knew it was untrue that we had been prevented from corresponding, or that there was any likelihood of such a ban in the future: but, thinking I might have read it and taken it as a sinister prophecy, he put on his hat and coat and came to the prison to reassure me.

'Old George' had the reputation of being quite a martinet, but his spontaneous act of kindness in leaving his fireside and hurrying to my cell on this errand showed another side of his character. I was most grateful for his reassurance, and told him I certainly wasn't going to fret about such nonsense. Unfortunately, though, the story would very likely cause distress to both Bunty's and my own close relatives and friends. He immediately gave orders that I was to be issued with two extra letters right away so that I could write and tell them not to worry, as that particular journalist was way out with his facts—or, rather, his conjectures.

One morning whilst the Deputy Governor was doing his rounds he beckoned me to come out of the workshop and told me I'd be leaving Durham in the near future and would be going to Maidstone. I suppose I should have felt elated by this news but somehow it left me cold. You get into a frame of mind in prison that the only thing which matters is the passage of time, no matter how strict the régime is. The mind gets lazy. Doing anything out of the ordinary routine requires a great effort—like the hill-billy's dog which lay on a thorn and was too lazy to move off it and get comfortable. I hadn't wanted to go to Durham, and never in my worst dreams had it occurred to me that I'd be sent there; but now I knew my days there were numbered I was unmoved—even though I was aware that Maidstone prison had a good reputation for a freer atmosphere than most.

The thing which did please me was that in my ignorance I took it for granted that Bunty would also be moved out of the Security Wing at Holloway. This was not to be: she remained confined in that Wing for another nineteen months, for reasons known only to the authorities.

Also in my ignorance I had assumed that the heat was off and that in Maidstone I'd be treated the same as any other prisoner. I ought to have known better by now. Though I wasn't dressed like Harlequin I was still treated as something out of the ordinary. For the first six weeks I was not put into a workshop and in fact had hardly any work to do at all: there was a bathroom in the Wing to which I had been allocated, and in conjunction with two other prisoners my sole task was to clean the place up in the mornings. The rest of the day was spent in wandering around inside the locked wing or sleeping. More freedom of movement was permitted in Maidstone than, I would imagine, in any other prison. There was a system whereby selected prisoners were given blue brassards and could escort up to six other prisoners from place to place. These selected 'Blue Bands', as they were called, failed to cotton to the fact that whilst they were escorting prisoners, the warders paid to do this very job were sitting back drinking tea and reading the papers. There was no shortage of volunteers to do the warders' work for them: we had a special name for such folk in the Navy.

Every time I left the Wing I had to be personally conducted by a warder with a black book containing my photograph and description. He signed for me in this book, and when we reached our destination he had to get another signature to say that I had arrived. After thirty months of this I came to regard myself more as a parcel or registered letter than as a human being. This pointless discriminatory treatment was certainly not imposed because of the nature of my crime: violent sexual offenders and murderers walked freely around the prison with blue bands on their arms—men who were capable, if they escaped, of repeating their crimes, which could hardly have been said about me. There was in fact a member of the Richardson torture gang in Maidstone who didn't have to suffer the indignity of being signed for: he was treated in exactly the same manner as other prisoners.

In spite of the relaxed atmosphere, or just possibly because of it, Maidstone was the only place in which I suffered real physical violence from other prisoners. I was attacked several times by the nick's equivalent of bovver boys or skinheads, all of them having graduated to prison via Borstal training. These young yobs were recruited by a man old enough to be their father, whose grandiose plan when he got out was to take over London now that the Kray gang had been broken up. As a fringe member and errand boy of another notorious gang, also broken up now, he carried a certain prestige among the youngsters. He visualised himself as Mr Big, sitting back and letting these lads do the dirty work. As they'd all be released on different dates, Mr Big gave them the address of a pub they should frequent in South-East London until they could all get together and start operating at full strength.

God help London if that little lot ever got operating! Implicit obedience was to be the watchword if they wanted to remain in 'the firm'. Various tasks were given them so that they could prove their mettle, such as sabotaging machinery in the workshop, breaking windows, and so on. But after their would-be boss had ordered them to set fire to the workshop—an attempt which, in every sense of the word, misfired—the gang was broken up and dispersed to other prisons. Such was their intelligence that it never occurred to them that if the workshop was burnt down we'd all be put on much less pleasant work.

It was just before this attempted arson that Mr Big gave his orders to 'Do Harry because of what the Russians are doing to Gerald Brooke'. So I got it, being knocked down and kicked if I went to the lavatory when no instructor was about, and also being subject to a barrage of lead from the typesetting machines in the print shop. They didn't care two hoots about Gerald Brooke: it was just an exercise to prove what they could get away with right under the eyes of authority.

Mr Big's enmity towards me was almost certainly due to a joke I'd been unwise enough to make on one occasion. Not knowing that from the moment of my arrest in January 1961 my usefulness to the Russians had ceased for all time, he was under the impression that I was something of a special case: why, otherwise, should I be personally escorted by a warder and signed for wherever I went? Assuming I was still somehow connected with the KGB, he approached me one day with the suggestion that if ever they wanted anyone 'knocked off' in this country, he could fix it for a grand—£1,000—and would I please put his name forward? He was so dim that he didn't realise at first that I was taking the mickey when I called him a 'cut-price assassin' and warned him that James Bond would chuck him out of the Union if he heard about these rock-bottom rates for a murder job. Maybe, I suggested, he should offer his services to MI5. With that he got furious, and nothing I could say would placate him. I suffered for my flippancy.

Gordon Lonsdale's sentence had been remitted after he had served only three out of his 25-year stint. He was exchanged for the British spy, Greville Wynne. On 24th October 1969 the Krogers left England, not on parole but with the remainder of their sentences remitted when they were swapped for Gerald Brooke. Bunty and I remained. There were no swaps for us.

From time to time there had been reports in the Press and on the radio that we were to be granted parole. We'd have been less than human if we hadn't indulged in some wishful thinking that these reports had some substance in them. We met every requirement of the Act of Parliament that had brought the parole system into being and had completed the necessary one-third of our sentence before the Act came into force. Neither of us had been in trouble with the law previously, and would have no opportunity of repeating our offence even if we had been so minded. There is nothing in the rules stating that certain offences debar the prisoner from being considered, the main criterion being the prisoner's future: will he or she become a better citizen if granted release on parole? In general the system has worked admirably: few have abused it, and Home Office figures show only a small percentage of failures.

We were entitled to three annual interviews by the Local Parole Committee, who make their recommendations to the Parole Board proper. On each occasion I had a very fair interview with a member of the local committee. I couldn't fault their impartiality: they were genuinely concerned with my future rather than with my past, and although of course they didn't tell me what their recommendations would be I had every reason to be satisfied that they had given me a full opportunity of putting my views forward. Whatever those recommendations may have been, however, parole was refused on the first two occasions by Lord Stonham. He had been dubbed the Prisoner's Friend when in Opposition, but now that he was a Minister of State for Home Affairs, with special responsibility for prisons, his friendship seemed to have waned.

My second opportunity of being released on parole would have been 30th March 1969, for which I was interviewed at Maidstone on 20th January 1969, leaving plenty of time for a decision to be reached and notified to me by the end of March. The date came and went, without a word. April came and went, and still no news. Then May, June, July, August, September...October.

The Krogers went, as I've said, in October. Still no word about Bunty or me.

It was not until 4th November, more than seven months after the date when we could reasonably have been released, that I received a billet-doux from the Minister of State to the effect that my application for parole had not even been referred to the Parole Board. These mental torturers in the Home Office were really excelling themselves.

Still there were Press reports of our imminent release. So many ambiguous statements were made that we didn't know what to believe. In my darker moments I even began to wonder—and still wonder—whether the Home Office was stringing us along in the hope that in desperation either or both of us would commit some major breach of prison discipline which would enable them justifiably to refuse us parole on grounds of misconduct. We had seen these tactics used on other people for different reasons, so we took good care not to fall into the trap.

In the meantime, just before I even got the result of my previous application I was interviewed for my next possible parole date—30th March 1970. This was rubbing it in a bit too much.

When refusal of parole became known to our local MP, Evelyn King, he raised the question of Bunty's continued detention during an adjournment debate in the House of Commons, and whilst he achieved no positive results there and then he did succeed in publicising the unfairness of her situation.

At last on 13th April 1970 we were informed that we were to be released on parole on 12th May. The cat and mouse game had ended.

No sooner had I been given the news by the Governor at Maidstone than the BBC and the Press were informed by the Home Office. This unprecedented step was the cause of acute harassment to both of us. Never before, apart from the statement in Parliament that the Krogers were to be exchanged for Gerald Brooke, had an announcement been made in advance of the release date of any prisoner in England. They intended to subject us to the same full glare of publicity coming out as we'd suffered before going in.

All the concession we got for more than nine years' exemplary conduct was ten months' parole on a 15-year sentence.

It is the rule that long-term prisoners due to be released on parole should have a preliminary weekend's leave to assist in rehabilitation, getting used to handling money, finding their way around unescorted, and seeking accommodation if they have no home to return to after all this time. One needs to get used to a thousand things outside prison which never impinge on one inside. Both Bunty and I expected this leave in order to re-orientate ourselves but, true to form, it was refused. I left prison having had no idea until four days previously where I was going to sleep on the night of my release. The cottage had been sold long ago, and the money paid into my account. I had had to state the district where I proposed to go, and the Senior Probation Officer of that area booked me temporary accommodation at a hotel for three nights until I could find somewhere to settle.

When a person is arrested he is, by the very nature of things, snatched off the street or taken from his home at a moment's notice. He is slung into a cell without any chance of settling his private and domestic affairs. All this has to be handled for him by others, some trustworthy and some very far from it. It comes as a great shock to many who emerge from prison, purged of the past and anxious to believe that everything now must go better, to find that most of their prized possessions have somehow disappeared or been disposed of by their trusted custodians. Some friends and relations try to make the path easy; others have already callously pulled a large part of it out from under your feet.

In this bewildering outside world I was apt at first to take people at their face value in the same way I had done before going to prison. I soon learned my mistake. It took me exactly four days to discover that the worst rogues are by no means all in prison.

Chapter Fourteen

It's Cold Outside

On the day I was due for discharge from Maidstone, I had a taxi sent into the prison. The driver had in the past taken me to see Bunty in Holloway, and once I asked him if he'd be prepared to help me dodge the newshounds when at last I was released. He promised to get me to London, and we fixed a price.

The taxi got into the prison all right, but it wasn't going to be so easy to get out. The Chief Officer warned me that reporters and TV cameras were massing outside.

'If you get past that lot, Harry, you'll be bloody lucky.'

We decided that I would lie on the floor of the cab, and the Chief Officer put a blanket over me. The driver took the Maidstone taxi identification plates off, and we drove out. I was treated to a running commentary as we went.

'We're out of the gate now...don't think they've spotted us... turning left...they don't know...oh, my God, somebody's on to us...' We went round side streets, back streets, in and out, whizzing around to shake them off. The driver managed it at last—save for one. It was a photographer, he told me, in an MG.

I couldn't stand much more of it under the blanket, so I said: 'Just one more go. Turn down a side street and see if you can shake him this time. If not, we'd better stop.'

The MG wasn't to be fooled. We stopped, and waited for it to come up.

I showed myself at the window. 'If I let you have a picture, will you get off my back?'

He agreed. In fact he took four or five, then honoured his word and cleared off.

All the rest of the Press boys, cottoning on that by now I was well away by car, hared off to Waterloo station. They took it for granted that I'd be showing up at Waterloo on my way to Portland. The only person who knew my real destination was the Chief Officer, who had made out my rail warrant, and he played it straight and didn't let out one single peep.

Even the driver didn't know my plans. After we'd disposed of the photographer and were on our way again, I said: 'We're not going to Waterloo.'

'But you said Waterloo.'

'I'm paying, aren't I?'

'Sure. Where *are* we going, then?'

'Clapham Junction.'

I got on a train at Clapham with my warrant made out to Poole, having been told I'd have to change at Surbiton. A porter there said there'd be two hours to wait, so I went out, walked around—feeling very shaky—and tried to adjust to the newness of it all. So many things were different even at first glance. Clothes had altered, prices had altered, cars and shop signs, the whole look and feel of the world had changed incredibly over the years. I bought some pyjamas. On discharge I had been given a suit, shirt, pair of shoes, raincoat and tie; but they weren't quite my style, and I gave them away to charity as soon as I could buy myself something that fitted.

Back at the station, there were still no pursuers. I got on the train, and by the time I reached Poole I was pretty sure I was all right.

At Poole I had to go over a high-level bridge. By now I was whacked, more from emotion than from physical exertion. You've no idea what it feels like to come out into the bustling world and have to cope for yourself—even coping with the simple business of getting on and off a train, reading notices, climbing a flight of steps is terrifying. After years of privation of every kind, with only enough food to keep you ticking over—and that of a quality to make you throw up—you feel too feeble to put one foot in front of the other.

I staggered over the footbridge and down the steps.

And there were the cameras.

Apparently the penny had dropped a bit late. Some of them at last got round to checking at Clapham, and a porter remembered someone answering my description asking about trains to Poole and being told about a wait at Surbiton. They had thereupon belted off to Poole to form a welcoming committee for me when I got there.

Photographs were gleefully taken of me tottering down the last couple of steps, and then they all started shouting questions.

Chivvied from all sides, I had literally to make a run for it, though I was in no condition for sprinting. I dashed towards a taxi, and got him started before giving him the address of the hotel which the Senior Probation Officer had fixed for me.

After we had been going for a minute or two I asked if there was anyone chasing us.

'About four cars,' he said.

'Don't go to the hotel, then. Drive to the nearest police station.'

'What's up?' He was beginning to get worried. 'You done anything?'

As we were following the one-way system to reach the police station, I saw a sign indicating the Probation Officer's entrance. 'Stop!' I said. 'I want to go there!' We had overshot by this time, so had to go once more round the block before I could be set down at the office. The Press boys were still on my heels.

The Senior Officer I'd been hoping to see was at Dorchester. His assistants realised I was nearly all in, and did everything they could for me. They certainly kept the Press boys out. It was a siege. I couldn't get out, but they weren't allowed in.

The Senior Probation Officer got back from Dorchester about an hour and a half later. I asked if I could ring my London solicitors before going a step further, and he agreed. When I made the call, there was great relief at the other end. They had been wondering where I was. As soon as they knew the date of my impending release, they had started negotiations for an exclusive interview which would not only put some money in my pocket but ensure that only one newspaper or agency dealt with me direct, so that I wouldn't have to run the gauntlet of all the assorted cameramen and newshounds who chose to crowd in on me.

A certain independent agency dealing in syndication rights had now offered Bunty and myself £750 each for exclusive rights in the handling of our story. The treatment was to consist in the main of a few pictures and an account of our first meeting after being released. Over the phone I agreed to this, but told the solicitor I was stuck in this office, already blockaded by a host of newspapermen. He got in touch with the agency and found they were sending a reporter and photographer by helicopter from London to Hurn Airport outside Bournemouth. I was to sit tight and make no statement at all to anyone else. He concluded by asking me to phone him in the morning so that we could discuss how things were working out.

Eventually the two men arrived. They didn't confront their rivals but found a back way into the building. Couldn't we all get out the same way? The probation officers and police leaned over backwards to help. They got me out through the police station itself to a waiting taxi, and this time we succeeded in evading the others.

The three of us—reporter, photographer and myself—needed somewhere to settle in and be quiet. The hotel booked for me in Poole was far too close to the Probation Office: we'd be spotted in no time. We drove off across Bournemouth, and finally plumped for the Pacific Hotel, now unfortunately closed. A few pictures were taken, and we discussed the programme.

All those years inside, one of the things Bunty had missed most of all was her early evening glass of sherry, and often in her letters to me she had said that when she got out what she most wanted was to sit down quietly and pour herself a glass. I now sent her a bottle of sherry with a message from me that only she would understand, to prove that suggestions for a meeting weren't all part of a put-up job on the part of the creatures who had been pursuing her.

This was a Tuesday. We arranged to meet on the Friday. The agency persuaded me to do rather more than had been asked for in the first instance, and I gave BBC and ITV interviews. Then, on the Friday, Bunty was brought out of her house over the back wall, while the rest of the Press still clustered on shift-work at the front.

We met at a rendezvous in the New Forest. They took pictures of Bunty and myself holding hands—all carefully posed, with instructions as detailed as though we were making a TV commercial... which is about the category it came into, I suppose. The BBC and ITV also showed up in the New Forest to record interviews.

Bunty was then driven home, finding to her relief that the Press, discovering she had flitted and not knowing how far or for how long, had given up and gone away.

On Tuesday our solicitor had told me to phone him the next morning. There had been so much going on that I hadn't been given the opportunity. When the reporter wanted me to go out with the photographer so they could get some pictures taken and sent off on the train in time for the London evening paper, I mentioned the call I ought to be making, and he promised to handle it for me. When we got back, he said he and my solicitor had had a chat, and there were no problems at all.

It wasn't until the Friday, after it was all over, that I got round to making a call myself.

'Where've you been?' was the instant reaction. 'We've been trying to get in touch with you. We've been conned.'

It appeared that, having got all they wanted, the agency had no intention of paying one penny of the promised money.

'But why didn't you pass some sort of message on when that chap rang you Wednesday morning?'

I knew as soon as I asked it what a stupid question it was. The reporter hadn't even rung them. He was still on the premises, so I steamed off and asked what the hell he'd been up to. But of course he was as innocent as a new-born babe, the way all reporters are when *you* start asking the questions.

That evening the agency boss himself came down and took me out to a meal to discuss things. The agency would generously pay my hotel bill for three days, and that would be the lot. I could have clouted him there and then but, having been out on probation for only a few days, that wouldn't have done me much good.

We could have taken civil action. Our solicitor assured us that we would win. But that sort of action takes money—there'd be no Legal Aid in such a case—and most of the money would undoubtedly go into the pockets of the only people who can't lose—the lawyers.

So this was our welcome when we emerged from prison into the land of decent, law-abiding citizens.

The papers who hadn't been able to get at me and hadn't done a deal with the agency naturally lost no opportunity of concocting some nasty stories of their own about me—and, even more and with a lot less reason, about Bunty.

The Press nearly drove Bunty round the bend. Their usual excuse is that their antics are in the public interest, and that freedom of the Press is one of our fundamental liberties. But how can it be in the public interest, and what high principles are involved, that someone emerging from over nine years in prison and in need of a spell of peace in which to readjust should be mercilessly hounded twenty-four hours a day? The sentence has been served: why should they make the outside world as big a hell as the 'inside' one?

Bunty was all alone in her house. Relatives and friends wanted to come and stay with her, to do anything they could for her. But she was determined to face it on her own. I offered to move in and fight people off; but she wouldn't have it.

On the second day she decided that she would go out shopping. She had been a prisoner long enough. Whatever was waiting, she'd face it.

A procession followed her all the way. Nearly everyone who actually spoke to her was nice and welcoming. But the ones who got into print were, of course, those with something vicious to say. There were reports in some papers about shopkeepers who had vowed not to serve her, and people who were prepared to curse her when they met her. She faced them courageously, and there were very, very few curses. It is significant that the few stories of her being shouted at in the street appeared in newspapers which had tried and failed to get exclusive stories from us as soon as we left prison; and remarkable that a photographer should be right on the spot just as someone stepped forward to shout, and remarkable that the words could be so clearly and accurately recorded.

What counted for far more than that was the pile of letters which Bunty received. There were so many it was impossible to reply individually. Only a tiny handful were malicious. I read them with her, and I destroyed them. The spontaneous kindness and encouragement were what meant most.

I stayed on at the hotel for a while, and the proprietor and his wife did everything in their power to make me comfortable, and valiantly kept the Press and unexpected visitors at bay. But I couldn't go on spending money on living in a hotel for much longer. When it was known that I was looking round for accommodation, the chambermaid suggested a reputable local agency, and I went along there with the Senior Probation Officer. I was given the address of a large house in which I might rent a flatlet, on the outskirts of Poole—a house right on the border between Poole and Bournemouth, in fact, which was to prove comically significant before very long.

Bunty was still in her old home on Portland. I used to visit her, leaving the car in a nearby car park and getting in the back way. Usually I arrived in the dark and left in the dark.

We were getting to know each other again, and we wanted to do this without the glare of the spotlight on us. It was understood between us that we were going to get married, but after what we'd been through we needed time to get our breath back. The Press went on niggling away: were we going to get married, or weren't we; was it true that Miss Gee hated me; was this true, was that likely . . .?

Bunty went occasionally to see her aunt and cousin in Worthing, and might be away for a week or two at a time. She never told a soul in Portland where she was going or who she'd be seeing. Each time the Press noticed that the house was empty they came haring round to my flatlet to ask where Miss Gee was, and to start up all the old questions again. Naturally I told them nothing. What I wouldn't have minded knowing was how they found my address anyway.

Then the house in which I was living came up for sale. Bunty and I decided to put together what money we had, and buy the place. It needed a lot doing to it, but we could do the work by stages and keep ourselves fairly comfortably by letting off flatlets as my previous landlady had done.

And we fixed a date for a quiet wedding at Poole Register Office.

It all went off smoothly, without anyone having the foggiest idea that we were now man and wife.

Now we had to get Bunty's furniture from Portland to our new address. There hadn't been much of mine to move. Although it was supposed to have been in safe keeping while I was away, most of it had vanished when I came to claim it. I seemed always to be arriving at or returning to a flat or house without a stick of furniture in it! Where that sort of thing's concerned, I must be accident prone.

The appearance of removal vans outside Bunty's house was bound to cause comment. It took only a few minutes for a local reporter to roll up in his car and park on the other side of the road. Fortunately for us, he was greedy. If he hadn't been so keen to cope with the story single-handed and win himself a scoop, but had called in a few colleagues, between them they could probably have followed every thread and so got the whole picture. As it was, he found himself painfully involved in a four-way stretch.

The house was on a slope. The removal vans parked tail to tail, one facing uphill and one downhill. I was in the house with Bunty when the men began to carry stuff out, and as we went along to keep an eye on some special items which needed careful packing, she spotted the watcher. I told her to keep her head turned away so that he couldn't get a photograph.

My car, too, was parked on the other side of the road. How were we to get to it and to the house in Poole without him giving chase and tracking us down?

In the end, Bunty decided to walk off up the road as though leaving the scene of all the activity. At the corner she stopped for an instant and waved to me. I waved back. The moment she was round the corner, she dashed down towards the back of the house and came in again that way.

The reporter didn't know which way to jump. Bunty had

apparently gone, but I was still there, and the vans were still loading.

We kept out of sight. The vans finished loading. Up went their tailboards. And then, to make the reporter's life still more wretched, one went off up the slope while the other headed in the opposite direction.

To add a final touch, I went out of the front door and crossed to my car. Then I turned to wave at the empty house, which must have baffled him yet further. He thought Bunty had gone; yet now it looked as though she had come back without him noticing. What was he to do: stay and watch the house, follow one of the vans (and if so, which one), or follow me?

I drove down hill and round the corner. Bunty, who had quit the house once more by the back way, was waiting at the end of the alley. She jumped in and we went as fast as I could take us to the house in Poole.

The reporter decided to stay and watch the house, presumably in the hope of questioning Bunty about her eventual destination. I'm afraid he must have had a long wait.

The furniture reached Poole without anyone being any the wiser. Luckily the contractors had provided plain vans, so our perplexed watcher hadn't even been able to record the firm's name and get round to badgering them later.

Word of Bunty's disappearance soon got round. Once more the news men were on my back. They kept rolling up at the house, asking: 'Where's Miss Gee?' I wouldn't tell them a thing. Several of them, hoping to stir up some kind of drama, asked if I really knew where she was: had she quit altogether? I assured them that I did know where she was—'But I'm not telling you lot.' They didn't know that I was no longer merely a flatlet tenant in the house, and it never seems to have occurred to them that Bunty was there all the time. Nor did it occur to them, and I didn't bother to tell them, that she was no longer Miss Gee.

A few days later I went to Portland to collect some bits and pieces we'd left behind. All the little dogs came scurrying at my heels, obviously expecting to be led to Bunty. After a while, a bit fed up with this farce, I stopped, waited for them all to catch up, and said:

'Look, you can follow me as much as you like, but I'll never lead you to Miss Gee.'

They paid no attention. I went on at the head of the cavalcade. In Weymouth I stopped for a coffee. They all stopped, too, and came in.

'Come on, Harry—where is she?'

'You don't *know*, do you?' another one prodded.

On we went to Portland. When I got to the house, parked at the front door. I did some of the work I'd come to do, then nipped out of the back way and along the alley to a pub which was now run by an old friend who had once worked with me. When we'd had a chat and a drink, I returned along the street and in through the front door again, which caused a bit of a flap.

'Where've you been?'

I finished what I had to do, and drove back.

On the Saturday, Bunty wanted to go to Worthing again to see her cousin. How were we going to get her out of the house without her being set on by the crowd?

Maybe if I hadn't had the bitter experience of that sharp operator the moment we were out of prison, I might have played along a bit more with the Press boys. But after that little episode I wasn't going to feed them one little crumb.

We had put up with enough. I rang the police.

They wasted no time. A sergeant came over and chased the whole lot away.

Next day three of them were back, ringing the doorbell. As soon as I opened the door they chorused:

'Congratulations.'

'What?'

'Congratulations, Harry.'

'What are you talking about this time?'

One of them dug into his pocket and brought out a copy of our entry in the marriage register.

'All right,' I said. 'You can call it off now. We're married. Who's the one who found out—you...you...or you?'

The bright boy grinned sheepishly. 'Me.'

'You can go right to the top of the class,' I said. 'You stupid lot—you've all been checking on Bournemouth Register Office every day, haven't you?'

They nodded.

'Well, this house,' I said, 'is the first or second house in Poole.'

Again they nodded. They knew it *now*. It had taken four weeks for the realisation to dawn on one of them.

They took it in good part, and now we could all laugh over it. Next day the papers did the best they could with this somewhat belated revelation. 'It can now be disclosed...' Fine stuff about a secret marriage, and how we'd had egg and chips for our wedding breakfast—which I don't suppose pleased the manager of the very good Poole hotel where we had lunch.

It's all behind us now. I'm not resentful about the retribution I've had to endure. What I did was wrong. I've paid for it.

But I do not accept glib condemnation from men who have done their country at least as much damage as I might have done —and, over recent years, probably far more. Tens of thousands of self-righteous people have, in their own special but less spectacular way, worked against the country's welfare with devastating results. Among them I'd include every one of the strikers in the docks, the motor industry and the mines, who have wrecked our economy. And I will accept no criticism from those Council workers who were responsible for the dead remaining unburied and for mounting pollution, or for those electricity workers who, quite apart from causing factories to shut down when our economic health depended on them, allowed the elderly to sicken and die without heat or cooking facilities, and brought the work of doctors and surgeons to a dangerous halt.

Last of all, I am still resentful and always shall be on Bunty's behalf. What she said in the box about her belief in Lonsdale as an American, what she said about her money being her own and her shares and savings certificates legitimately bought, what she said about her not having realised what I'd dragged her into—all these things were true, but she was never given a chance to explain this, and no facilities were allowed for bringing the evidence which would have confirmed it. She really believed that justice in this country is pretty sound, even for people who have done wrong or simply been foolish. She didn't realise, and still finds it hard to grasp, that what we were exposed to wasn't justice but a propaganda exercise.

None of this alters the fact that I am deeply sorry for the part I played in the whole affair. After those grim years inside I shall certainly never transgress again: I wouldn't even ride a push-bike without lights.

During the debate on the Criminal Justice Bill in Parliament in 1967, the late Sydney Silverman said: 'No man ever came out of prison a better man than when he went in.' Remembering all too well the conditions under which a prisoner has to exist, and their long-term effects on him, I'm afraid the weight of the evidence supports Mr Silverman's gloomy view. But I'll do my best to prove him wrong.